T0128979

The World of Micronations

For those who are tired of existing incompetent governments and are longing for something new and refreshing

Mohammad Bahareth

iUniverse, Inc.
Bloomington

MICRONATIONS
FOR THOSE WHO ARE TIRED OF EXISTING INCOMPETENT GOVERNMENTS AND ARE LONGING FOR SOMETHING NEW AND REFRESHING

Micronations, First Edition
Part of the iSay Franshise

Author Website:
www.Bahareth.info

ISBN: 978-1-4620-6926-2 (sc)
ISBN: 978-1-4620-6927-9 (ebk)

Library of Congress Control Number: 2011961464

iUniverse books may be ordered through booksellers or by contacting:

iUniverse
1663 Liberty Drive
Bloomington, IN 47403
www.iuniverse.com
1-800-Authors (1-800-288-4677)

Printed in the United States of America

iUniverse rev. date: 12/21/2011

CONTENTS

Overview and Introduction

Ask any person whether they are interested in power and they are likely to deny it on your face. Many would like to use a politically correct term such as "servant leadership" or sharing their leadership qualities with other people. They will look at others and declare that they are power hungry; they themselves are men and women of noble motives.

There is something especially in men that seeks that top position and they will do anything to make sure they get it. You see it often in the animal kingdom where the stronger one of the any species assumes a leadership position. Talk about top—dogs or alpha males. This is what in our own political systems, where this love for power is often disguised as interest in the electorate's health care, education as well as other numerous responsibilities. None of these leaders will ever say I do this because I love power.

Power is a real hot potato, and those who seek it will always get a fitting terminology which will hide any underlying motives. Power in itself is good and the right use of the same always has many positive outcomes. Men love power so much that they will do anything to get hold of it. You should also see how men reach when they lose power. Bob Woodward and Carl Bernstein record President Nixon's reaction to his loss of power in the book, the Final Days: "Between sobs, Nixon was plaintive . . . How had a simple burglary . . . done all this? . . . Nixon got down on his knees . . . [He] leaned over and struck his fist on the carpet, crying, 'What have I done? What has happened?'"

Turning Dreams to Reality

Many times leaders have emerged because a number of people were not satisfied with the status quo. When people are not satisfied with how power is being exercised, there are many things that they can do. Whereas plenty of people support the policies of various governments, there are those who do not and will do anything to see a change of guard. The truth of the matter is that it is virtually impossible to please just about every one in the way power is exercised.

It could be that some people are dissatisfied with certain taxes or laws and when it is election time, they come out looking for leadership positions promising to change the way things are done. It is this desire that has given some people an idea of tailoring a government that could run exactly the way they want things to go. Sometimes the wish to make sure that the justice system, economic structures, national security, education and etc runs just like we want them to. The ability to tailor government structures in a specific unique regime runs in the blood of many people only that they do not know what to do about it.

Some people intent on developing a paradise of sorts look forward to being able to have a strict control on immigration policies, imports and exports, foreign relations, currency, defense programs and just about everything else that will run a government. Suppose you are in a position to plan things in government and they flow just like you desire? Suppose you had your own small country where things are efficient? What if in this imaginary country you would only move in with your closest buddies and close family members—that sounds like a very imaginative mind.

The truth of the matter is that there are people who got dissatisfied with the status quo and decided to take action. Yes! They started their own countries. The entities that are created may not necessarily fit the bill of your ordinary country but all the same they exist. There are several miniature countries around the world which operate like sovereign states. These residents and leaders live as if they were independent and some of them have the faintest hope that order of things will one day be recognized internationally. There are many cases where they even issue stamps, coins, and passports, and have a national anthem.

Finding Space for Your New Country

Of course the ordinary thinker will start contemplating where to find land to start a new political state because according to them all the land the world over has been occupied. Since all land appears to have been taken over any existing country will fight tooth and nail to keep their existing land. Not so for those who are intent on changing the nature of things—there many who have gone as far as declaring any little property they own and independent country.

You will of course have to deal with plenty of challenges on the way in order to make their dreams reality. People will declare private lands, apartments or even some tiny island a new country. You may have to also work hard to convince the jurisdiction from which you are operating that you just need to secede. Many people have created micro nations from artificial islands on any place on the planet or perhaps some floating ship anchored somewhere in international waters. Since such people are generally risk takers they will not worry that there entity may not be recognized by any other state.

How then will work in order to convince a few people you are not out of your mind so that they get to join you in the new country so that it becomes viable? Any republic will need a running government, security forces and not forgetting a system that will ensure the required provisions get to the population. Apart from cultivating the ability to produce enough to satisfy your regime's need, you will need to have an import and expert system which means such a country will need citizen with some income generation activities.

A great deal of thinking will also have gone to creating social systems such as schools, hospitals and many other social amenities or else your people will have to travel abroad to look for the same. Other systems that will need to be in place include police and court systems, infrastructure to do with electricity distribution, water and sewage services, a transport system as well as telephone and other communication services. When people think about these major challenges they almost always give up on the idea of creating a new state.

Even with all those complications, a few people have gone right ahead and founded micro nations, some of which have survived for quite an amount of time. There are those that tried and survived briefly only to shut down by invading bigger neighbors yet others have gone on to survive. There are all reasons why micro nations come up and similarly why some do not get to survive.

Apparently, where there is no land, there are those micro nations that survive only on the internet, this could be as a result of having some comic or artistic reasons, looking for publicity or even a political protest of sorts. You must have heard about virtual real estate where people live in imaginary countries and they survive in a lot of role playing. Whether you are looking at a virtual or real micro nation, this craze satisfies the desire by many people to live a better life, or perhaps one where you live according to your deepest desires and dreams. It may appear that sooner rather than later we will actually be talking about Nanonations.

Academic attention

In the recent past there has been some significant interest in the micronation phenomenon over the years. Many academicians have mainly been concerned about studying the seemingly anomalous legal satiations that surround such established micronations such as the Hutt River Province and the Sealand. It is believed that any of these emerging micronations represent some ideas inherent in the community and they provide an opportunity for role playing. Some of the ideas represented by micronations have very deep political undertones that need to be communicated.

Even though these entities may not be recognized by the United Nations there are many publications that have tried to address the subject. The New York Times carried an article in May 2000 entitled "Utopian Rulers, and Spoofs, Stake out Territory Online" and it is here that for the first time many people became aware of the existence of micronations. Many other newspapers have carried out similar publications bringing to the fore these micronations.

Micronational Territories and cultures

The fact that majority of these micronations remain unrecognized by the world's nation states and inter-government organizations has made it happen that they often operate as simulations. This is without any particular regard to the origin, themes and goals of any one of them. There are those that claim real territory somewhere on the planet and occasionally they will do so with intentions of seceding in order to authenticate their claims. However, many other micronations operate parallel with already existing nations though others will develop virtual worlds of their own.

More often than not these micronations interact with one another in a recognized diplomatic system. At other instances they move on with simulations of economic blue prints as well as war games. Many of them operate like they were a form of a political club but replicating the features of social networking. Others that have more complex simulations have gone on to create more complex role playing cultures in their own worlds.

Majority of these micronations have developed themes and cultures that are unique to themselves which can be based on historical or current nations. However, you should not be surprised when you realize they have come up with a unique invention of their own. They also operate in separate loose groups primarily defined by languages.

Chapter One

Welcome to the World of Micronations

There are many people who have never heard about the existence of micro nations. There are so many people who have created micro nations and they have gone on to survive.

And the process of creating one is not really rocket science. One only needs to convince a few neighbors or friends and assign themselves the presidency with a first lady to boot. A fence around the present borders and a system that will make stamps, visas, some currency and in these modern days a website and you are home and dry.

Micro Nations are just like your ordinary country only that some of them may not be recognized by any major states. There are also some that only exist in the creators minds whereas others exist only on paper or the virtual world. It may be a little difficult to know exactly where to place a micro nation when compared to real existing nations. A real nation has to have these four components in order to qualify to be one:

1) There should land where the nation exists

2) There must be a population

3) There should be a running government

4) There should be diplomatic relations with neighboring countries

Even though micro nations may have some of these qualities, in reality it I difficult to come across one that fulfill all the conditions of nationhood. Paradoxically there are other nations that fail in some of those areas as well but have been somehow recognized by other nations.

The oldest known micro nation in existence is said to be Talossa, which was apparently created by a teenager, 14 year old Ben Madison. Starting with just a few relatives in his bedroom it has grown to several hundreds of people known as Talossans and there is even a language—Talossan with a vocabulary of over 25,000 words. They are so patriotic that they even have an anthem and a Talossafet, to show you the kind of following it commands. Found on the East Side neighborhood in Milwaukee as well as the island of Cezembre and a portion of the Antarctica.

What is a Micro Nation?

A micro nation can actually be referred to as new country project or a model country. The definition of a micro nation is thus rendered:

"An entity that resembles a nation or a state, but which for the most part exists only on paper, on the Internet, or in the mind of its creator."

Also referred to as:

"Model countries and new country projects—are entities that claim to be independent nations or states but which are unrecognized by world governments or major international organizations."

Different reasons exist why micro nations are created some being extremely serious whereas others are as a result of a hobby. There are however very genuine micro nations which are made of an entire community or tribe. These small entities almost always exist as replicas of real nations as opposed to existing states. We can therefore say that these are small nations with a small geographical area as well as populations.

The term micro nation can also be used synonymously with the term Fifth nation which also refers to social identity groups. Compared to micronations are macronations which are significantly larger and enjoy some territorial recognition and these are referred to as Fourth world nations. You will find many secessionist or self determination groups counted among macronations.

It is also very easy to confuse micronations with those tiny nations that are recognized legitimately. These geographically small counties include countries such as Monaco, Fiji and San Marino. Micronations should not be confused with legitimately recognized, but geographically tiny nations such as Fiji, Monaco, and San Marino, for which the term microstate is more accurate and descriptive.

Common Micronation Features

You can identify a micronation easily by looking at the following features that can be sued to identify them.

- The form and structure they use is very similar to those of your every day sovereign republic such as claims to territory, official symbols, and citizenry as well as miniature government institutions.

- The populations and geographical areas are relatively small when compared to other nations and of course a form of citizenry as well.

- Formal structures that make the day to day running of business life such as bank notes, coins, postage stamps as well as travel documents are also available.

- Unlike entities such as tribes, clans, sects, community associations and campuses, micro nations usually demand recognition from the international community.

There have been some attempts to create a legally accepted definition that would differentiate between states and non—state entities and the Montevideo Convention was one such attempt. It is at this convention where it was emphasized that a state could actually exist without necessary being in possession of a definite territory. Micronations have also been referred to as fantasy country, model country, counter-nation, pseudo-nation, new country project, online nations, etc among others.

Mohammad Bahareth

History of Micronations

Even though micronation existed previously the current rebirth began between the 1960s and 1970s when a number of territorial micronations, some of which survive to date emerged. One of the most famous ones is the Principality of Sealand which was founded on an abandoned World War II gun platform in 1967. Located in the North Sea this micro nation has endured a number of military coups, rough weather as well as court rulings which threatened its existence. Some people even attempted to construct artificial islands but there has been minimal success here.

The following year 1968 saw the rise of the Republic of Rose Island which is a 400 square meter platform built in the Adriatic Sea off the Italian town of Rimini. Apart from managing to issue stamps it minted its own currency and also declares Esperanto its official language. It was however obliterated shortly after its completion by the Italian navy. Come 1972 Nevada businessman Michael Oliver founded the Republic of Minerva in a shoal located in the Pacific Ocean to the South of Fiji Island. After successfully creating an artificial island they lacked the support of getting international recognition. The adventure came to an end after the nearby Tonga sent a military force and forcefully annexed it.

There are younger participants to day who are apt to create micro nations based on their hobbies. The internet is abuzz with diverse communities and sectors that have given an outlet to those people who are intent in creating them. It may be a little difficult to establish the exact number of micro nations it may appear that there are more than 2000 in existence. The internet has made it possible for people to overcome those traditional challenges that made it impossible for them to create real micro nations. Many current micro nations are can actually be a one man affair whereas real time micro nations would coax several hundreds of people and grant them real citizenry.

Chapter Two

Categories of Micronations

We have established that micronations are forms of official nationhood only that they are the smallest that can become. Some of these nations hold very little land whereas there are those that hold none at all. However, most of them lay claim on sovereignty to some independent territory. Some are recognized and other are not recognized at all.

At the bottom of the matter, the issue with most micronations is the desire for people to found new countries. Most of them end up declaring dominion on land that exists somewhere while others choose tiny, isolated islands or some remote areas from where they launch their projects. With proclamations of independence, adopted constitutions, seeking for diplomatic recognition and sending of envoys, national flags, passports, stamps and currencies you can imagine how serious some of them can actually be.

There are different categories of micronations that range from tiny established and recognized states. A good example would be the island of Antigua that has a population of less than one hundred thousand people to other model nations, some of which boast the population of one citizen. There are major categories of micronations that can be discussed.

Established States

This category of micronations is usually referred to as Micro States that actually own well recognized sovereign land. They are more often than not recognized as independent states by several world countries. Some of the most popular of established micronations include independent islands such as Antigua as well as the Vatican City. The Vatican City is a state within the city of Rome that actually owns about 108 acres of sovereign land. Other forms of micronations look forward to having the status such as what these two microstates have.

States in Exile

This is a class of micronations that have running governments but they do not have or have lost claim to sovereign land. These are the micro states that could have been recognized as established at some point in the past. They have legitimate claims to a homeland and they are actually recognized by several major countries. A good example of a state in exile is the Tibetan government of the Dalai Lama. These types of exiled micronations extremely viable and have hope of achieving their goals. A fact many people know little about is that France existed as a micronation during the Second World War. It consisted of an organized faction that had apparently lost all its land to the German invasion.

Unrecognized Races and Tribes

This category of micronations, always referred to as 'unrecognized people', is usually composed of groups of political, racial and social factions who claim the need for their independence. Their reasons are that their unique needs are not met by the already existing and dominant national and political environment that prevails. Many of these unrecognized people will not have had their own government system in the past or may not have formed a form of central government in the past to try and replace a former government that could have ended in history.

Included in this category of micronations are a good number of modern Native American nations as well as a number of indigenous groups spread all over the world. One very successful example of a formerly "unrecognized people" is the modern nation of Israel. This nation was actually founder after the Second World War for the purpose of restoring the Hebrew people to their former homeland. This is despite the fact that the old time government of Israel had become obliterated after being in exile for such a long time.

Model States

There are people who are usually intent in proving their points and political ideas hence model states which can be said to be political science experiments. The range of model states is wide and includes attempts at establishing new landed nations to the extent of real hypothetical theories. It can be said that model states are not so serious attempts at trying to form new governments.

These microstates always exist as a working system of government consisting of several people who lay claim to some existing parcel of land and work at manifesting their sovereign status and recognition. There are several examples of model states but the most famous one is the nation of Oceana where there was an attempt to take over some abandoned ocean platforms off the British coast. Oceana actually managed to get recognition by several states and they even went on to issue passports and mint their own currency.

Imaginary States

This can be called the least serious model nations which do not have really proper goals for the establishment of real status. Talk about fantasy creations and you have these imaginary states in mind. The whole idea about them is more often than not fictional in terms of government, history, territory as well as language. In other instances imaginary states become a form of a game where role playing is the major theme with a large number of people participating. A most popular imaginary state is very well maintained by the Society for Creative Anachronism and declares baronies as well as supporting tournaments in medieval character

The modern world has seen the creation of extremely few landed nations. There are very few exceptions that could happen occasionally especially when nations get reorganized such as happened some time ago in South Africa. Since all land is under the control of already existing nations, most of them have tough policies that would not allow them to release even an inch of their land.

The existing micronations therefore can be said to be as a result of a compromise between the desires of people with strong feelings of having a separate nationhood and the willingness of major world countries. Many of these micronations can be said to be an attempt from some people manifest their own independence without trying to interfere with the existing state of affairs as far as nationhood is concerned. Where they are not tolerated they are systematically ignored by world governments and countries. Where they exist, they sometime do as substrata of human organization with less than fully recognized status.

Reasons Micronations are founded

Currently there are several reasons micronations are founded

Social, economic or political simulations

These appear to be the most serious looking of all micronations because more often than not they involve mature participants. They have highly developed structures in their day to day activities which very closely relate to the running of any regular world nation. There are several examples of such micronations that exist today and they include:

Freetown Christiania

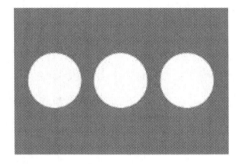

Flag of Christiania

Also known as Christiania this is a self proclaimed semi-independent neighborhood which as less than 1000 residents and covers an area that is about 85 acres in Christianshavn in Copenhagen. Its unique status was created be a special law that was adopted as the Christiania Law in 1989 and parts of the supervision for the district were transferred from the Copenhagen Municipality to this quasi-state.

Entrance to Christiania

There has been a lot of controversy regarding the creation of this district in a squatted military barrack. Cannabis was traded legally and the authorities could not tolerate it beyond 2004. Since then, measures for normalizing the legal status of the community have led to conflicts, and negotiations are on going. This is a quasi legal district found in Copenhagen, Denmark which was founded in September 1971. A unique feature in this micronation is the laxity of laws relating to drugs and squatting when compared to the rest of the world.

Talossa

Perhaps this is the best known political simulation which has gone so far as to even invent its own language, Talossan.

Talossa was founded in December 1979 by Ben Madison then known as the Kingdom of Talossa. Today there are three micronations that use that same name: two of them ore called the Kingdome of Talossa; Madison and Woolley Kingdoms and the third one is know as the Republic of Talossa.

The Holy Empire of Reunion

It was founded in Brazil in August 1997 this is a virtual constitutional empire simulation which has quite a number of members the entire world over.

Historical simulations

These second category of micronations appears to be only fairly serious and usually involve a good number of persons whose main interest is to try and recreate the past. Most of these people are mostly concerned about the Mediaeval or Roman past and they love to live it in an explicit way.

Nova Roma Micronation

This small group of just about 100 people was created way back in 1998. They have gone on to mint their own coins and they chiefly engage in trying to reenact a Roman themed life in real time.

Exercises in personal entertainment or self-aggrandizement

This happens to be the most common of all categories of micronations since there are literally thousands of them. They also happen to be the most short lived because they more often than not internet based micro nations. The people involved in any one of them are usually not too many and their main concerns would almost always be propagating the outward symbols of statehood according the founders terms and definitions.

They arrogate themselves by way of using grand sounding titles, honors, awards and a myriad of symbols that have their roots in ancient European traditions with their dominant form of manifestation being wars with other micronations. The current examples include:

The Aerican Empire

This micronation was founded in May 1987 and is best known for claiming swathes of land on so many planets. They even have a national flag which is smiley faced and they have quite a number of national holidays with strange names such as the 'Topin Wagglegammon'.

The Republic of Molossia

This tiny republic that was founded by Danny Wallace in January 2005 is an attempt by once person to create his won internet based republic from his own flat in London. He is the monarch who goes by the title King Danny I.

The Duchy of Bohemia

The Duchy of Bohemia was founded in 2007 and claims to be a micronation and government in exile and operates within the borders of USA. The founders claim that it is a continuation the ancient Kingdom of Bohemia which happens to be the last dynasty to be relinquished by the Holy Roman Emperors.

Exercises in fantasy, creative fiction or artistic expression

This category of micronations are usually a product of fertile imaginations that are basically stand alone artistic projects mainly based on online and offline fiction. Some of them are also creations from popular films and novels and they abound in plenty. Some very prominent examples include:

San Serrife

This is among the best April fool's day hoaxes ever created by a British Newspaper. The Guardian produced a 7 page intricate supplement which has been subject to revisiting by several newspapers ever since then.

Lizbekistan

This is an internet based creation of Australian artist Liz Stirling which was founded sometime in 1987.

Ladonia

Swedish historian and artist Lars Vilks is said to have founded the micronation of Ladonia in June 1996 and he has territorial claim on a piece of land in Southern Sweden.

Vehicles for the promotion of an agenda

Political and social reformers are also not left behind in the pursuit for the formation of micronations. Whereas the existence of some of these micronations is simply maintained by the media others are a mere public relations exercise. Typical micronations of this category include:

Akhzivland

This self declared 'independent republic' was established way back on the 1950s by an Israeli ex-sailor Eli Avivi on the Mediterranean Beach at Akhviz in Israel. He went on to declare it an independent state in 1970.

The Conch Republic

Interesting as it may seem this micronation was started as a form of protest by business owners and residents of Florida Keys in April 1982.

The Gay and Lesbian Kingdom of the Coral Sea Islands: As the name suggests this micronation was founded on an uninhabited Coral Sea Island off the coast of Queensland, Australia in June 2004. The founding of this particular micronation was in response to the Australian government's refusal to recognize same sex marriages.

Entities created for fraudulent purposes

There are a number of micronations which have also been created for fraudulent purposes as well. These are used to link dubious or unlawful illegal transactions with nations that appear to be legitimate. There are a large number of these and some of them include:

The Dominion of Melchizedek

In 1986 a father and son team of con artists and confident tricksters known as Evan David Peldley and Ben David Pedley created the Dominion of Melchizedek for the sole purpose of selling fake banking licenses. They claimed that Melchizedek was an "ecclesiastical constitutional nation" that laid claim on a number of territories as well as a large portion of the Antarctica. Apparently many people associated with the Dominion of

Melchizedek have been convicted and indicted for a number of crimes.

The Kingdom of EnenKio

This is one micronation that has received condemnation for selling passports as well as diplomatic papers from the government of Marshal Islands as well as USA. It claims the Wake Toll Island that belongs to those Minor Outlying Island of the United States. Their fraudulent machinations were condemned in a circular from the Foreign Affairs Ministry of the Republic of Marshal Island in 1998. The circular also included the aforementioned Melchizedek Dominion as fraudulent.

The United Kingdom of Atlantis

The United Kingdom of Atlantis operated a website for two years beginning October 2003 to 2005 with claims that it was located in the neighborhood of Australia in the Pacific Ocean. They even went further to publish maps of the alleged location but the truth of the matter was that the islands did not just exist. It later emerged that the leader of Atlantis, Sheikh Yakub Al-Sheikh Ibrahim was a man on the run who was wanted by the US authorities for crimes that included money laundering and fraud. There are records that indicate that at one time Atlantis sent an "official" delegation to the State of Palau with offers of a low interest loan of $100 million.

Historical anomalies and aspirant states

Another category of micronations are those that are founded on genuine aspirations of people to become a sovereign state. This may be as a result of historical injustices or simply peculiar interpretations of the law and they can be very easily confused with existing established states. You are likely to find these micronations on unusually small but often disputed territorial communes. They more often than not generate some income of their own through economic activities such as sale of stamps, tourism and numismatic sales. Most other nations almost always tolerate them or at worst they simply behave as if they don't exist. There are a number of examples such as:

The Principality of Sealand

It calls itself a "sovereign principality" which was established in September 1967. Its location is in the North Sea on a Second World War anti-aircraft gun platform and what you would say are international waters. Currently controversy is brewing between the United Kingdom and Sealand regarding the ownership of those territorial waters. A business calling itself HavenCo is based in Sealand; it is a collocation site that promises total security to customers' data which they claim is secure from any kind of legal action.

The Hutt River Province Principality

This one is a based on a farm in Western Australia that claims to have seceded from Australia in April 1970 to become an independent principality and claims to have a world citizenship of over 13,000 people.

The Independent Long Island movement

This micronation was founded in August 2007 on the Long Island which was British from 1674 following the Westminster Treaty. This treaty made the Long Island part of the British colony of New York and remained so during the entire American Revolution War of 1775 to 1783. It was only evacuated in 1783 following the Treaty of Paris. Since Long Island is a naturally uninhabited island it has all the rights accorded to natural uninhabited and independent islands as governed by the international law.

Exercises in historical revisionism

Wolfgang Gerhard Guenter Ebel founded the Kommissarische Reichsregierung in Berlin in 1985 asserting that the ancient Germanic Empire, also known as Prussia still exists in its pre-World War II era. Also known as KRR or provisional Imperial Government in English this grouping includes numerous groups who want to see the return of the Ancient Germany borders and they consider themselves its government in exile. There are more than sixty people or organizations that are currently said to be associated with KRRs.

New-country projects

There are people who have novel ideas who actually attempt to create completely new nations by trying to construct artificial islands. Even though very few if any have ever seen the light of the day, a big percentage of them claim to embrace libertarian or democratic principles of the highest order. There have been several attempts and a few prominent ones include:

The Republic of Minerva

The founders of this Libertarian project actually succeeded in constructing a miniature man made island on the Minerva Reefs located south of Fiji in 1971 and went on to declare it an independent state in January 1972. The independence was however short lived because they got ejected by troops from Tonga and by June 15th 1972 it was formally annexed. Later, in November 2005 the government of Fiji forwarded a complaint with the International Seabed Authority claiming ownership of the Minerva Reefs.

The Principality of Freedonia

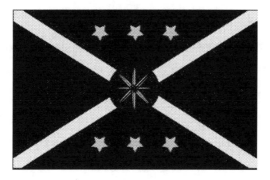

This libertarian project was established in 1992 by a group of US teenagers as a hypothetical project before it finally became a new country project in 1997. They even went ahead and tried to lease land from the Sultan of Awdal in Somaliland in January 2001. The resultant public dissatisfaction led to a riot during which a Somali national was reported to have died.

Seasteading

People intent in making a completely new lifestyle in the oceans abound; the intention is usually to make a new home in a sea going craft—this is what is called Seasteading. Historically, Seasteds have been sailing crafts as can be seen demonstrated by the Chinese Junk, modified canoes in Oceania or the Pirates of Libertaria. Current theoretical seasteds have the idea of using floating platforms through which people can create sovereign micronations which they believe could end issues to do with ocean colonization. This is a concept that is believed to have been introduced by Wayne Gramlich who later wrote a book about it with Patri Friedman and Andy House.

There is still a lot of research and experimentation going on about the entire concept of Seasteading with issues regarding the economic, social as well as political aspects being taken into consideration. Seasteds will have potential business ventures such as offshore aquaculture, casinos, and data havens together with the gamut of business endeavors. These seaborne platforms will be plying international waters with completely new communities.

Chapter Three

List of the Smallest Microstates

A microstate is actually a sovereign state that is fully recognized by all other world nations but has a very small land area or population but more often than not it is both. There are several Mini-states with the smallest of them all being the Vatican City, which had a population of less than 900 residents as of July 2010 and it covers a total area of only 0.44 square kilometers.

It is important to note that a microstate is not a micronation. Most micronations are not recognized as official states. There are other territories that lack full sovereignty that do not qualify to be called microstates either. Such areas include British Crown Dependencies, Administrative Regions and territories abroad belonging to the Netherlands, France, Denmark, United Kingdom as well as Norway.

A good number of these microstates were founded on historical anomalies or peculiar interpretations of the law. Most of these microstates are mostly located on tiny territorial enclaves and most of their economic activities are founded on tourism, philatelic and other related activities.

Following is a list of the world's smallest independent countries beginning from the tiniest of all.

Vatican City

Also known as the Holy See, Vatican is the world's smallest state covering an area of only 0.2 square miles. It has a population of less than 900 people and actually none of them is a permanent resident. This miniature country surrounds the St. Peter's Basilica which is the headquarters of the Roman Catholic Church.

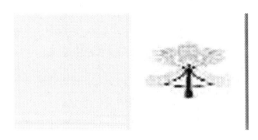

St. Peter's Basilica

The Vatican City is a land locked sovereign city-state with a walled territory in a small enclave within the city of Rome. The entire land they occupy is approximately 110 acres. Vatican was established in 1929 by the Lateran Treaty that brought the city-state into existence and is ruled by the Bishop of Rome who is also called the pope. Its highest functionaries are catholic clergymen from various nations the world over.

Monaco

Monaco covers an area that is only 0.7 square miles and lies along the French Riviera near the City of Nice in the Mediterranean. This is the second smallest country in the world and it has a population of slightly over 32,000 people. Monaco is known especially for its Monte Carlo Casinos and Princess Grace.

It is also the world's smallest monarchy with the highest population density in the world. There is little geographical distinction between the City and State of Monaco even though both have different responsibilities in running the state.

Nauru

Flag of Nauru

This island of close to 10,000 residents in the Pacific was formerly known as Pleasant Island and became independent in 1968. Its nearest neighbor is Banaba Island in Kiribati which is some 186 miles to the east. This is the world's smallest island nation covering an area that is only 8.5 square kilometers. It is also the second least populated country after the Vatican City.

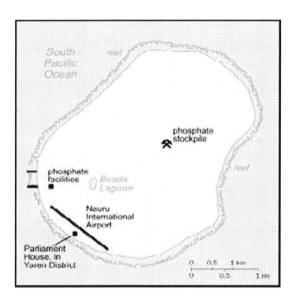

Nauru is a phosphate rock island which has deposits very close to the surface which allows for simple strip mining. It has been a major exporter of phosphate since as early as 1907 only that the deposits ran out in the 1980s. Nauru boasted one of the greatest per-capita incomes during the 1960s and 1960s.

Tuvalu

Initially known as Ellice Island, Tuvalu is the fourth smallest country in the world, being only bigger than Vatican City, Monaco and Nauru; it covers an area that is 9 square miles and is composed of 9 coral atolls which gained independence in 1978. It is home to close to 12,000 people making it the third least populous state in the world.

The Polynesian island nation found in the Pacific Ocean is found midway between Hawaii and Australia with neighbors such as Samoa, Fiji, Kiribati and Nauru. It comprises of reef islands and five coral atolls which voted for separate British dependency status as Tuvalu in 1974. This separated it from what was formerly called Gilbert Islands which later became Kiribati on gaining independence. Tuvalu became the 189th member of the United Nations on September 5, 2000.

San Marino

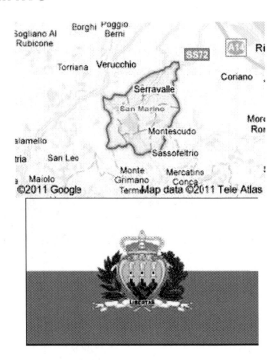

The Most Serene Republic of San Marino which is home to close to 29,000 people is located on Mt. Titano in Northern Italy claims to be the oldest European country founded in the fourth century. This tiny enclave surrounded by Italy occupies some 24 square miles. It has the smallest population of all the members of the Council of Europe.

San Marino is actually the oldest surviving sovereign state being a continuation of a community founded on September 3rd, 301. This country has a constitution that was enacted in 1600 and it must be the oldest constitution that is still in effect the world over. San Marino has an extremely stable economy with the lowest unemployment rate in the entire European continent as well as no national debt and always has a budget surplus.

Liechtenstein

This microstate that is home to over 35,000 people is said to be the smallest yet wealthiest German speaking country in the world and it's the only country that lies entirely in the Alps. It is a doubly land locked country that is bordered by Switzerland to the South and West and Austria to the East. It measures some

62 square miles and has the second highest GDP per person in the world.

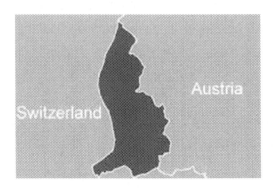

Location of Liechtenstein

Liechtenstein also happens to be the only predominantly German speaking country that does not share a single border with Germany. Much of the terrain in this constitutional monarchy is mountainous and that makes it a favorite spot for winter sports.

It is the only predominantly German-speaking country not to share a common border with Germany. It is a constitutional monarchy divided into 11 municipalities. Much of Liechtenstein's terrain is mountainous, making it a winter sports destination. Its landscape is characterized by many small farms and cultivated fields that dot the landscape to the north and the south. It has been identified as a tax haven because of the strong financial sector it has in its capital Vaduz. Liechtenstein is a member of the European Free Trade Association as well as the European Economic Area.

Marshall Islands

Marshall Islands gained independence in 1986 and were formerly a part of the Trust of Pacific Islands which was administered by the United States. It covers an area that is estimated to be 70 square miles with a population of close to 34,000 people. It consists of several atolls, reefs and 34 islands.

Saint Kitts and Nevis

The flag of Saint Kitts and Nevis

The federation of Saint Kitts and Nevis is a Caribbean country that gained its independence in 1983 and is home to about 39,000 people. It covers an area that is 104 square miles and of the two islands, Nevis is the smaller one and has a guaranteed right to secede should it feel like so. This federal two island nation is found in the Leeward Islands in the West Indies.

Saint Kitts and Nevis is the smallest state in the Americas both in area as well as population. Originally it had the British Dependency of Anguilla in its union that was known as Saint Christopher—Nevis—Anguilla. Saint Kitts and Nevis are among the very first islands in the Caribbean that attracted European settlers with Saint Kitts being the first French and British Colonies in the Caribbean area.

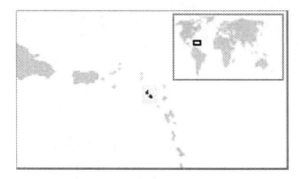

Location of Saint Kitts and Nevis

Seychelles

Seychelles is an island country located in an Indian Ocean archipelago consisting of 115 islands located some 932 miles off mainland Africa. It has a population of 86,000 people and gained independence in 1976. It covers some 107 square miles and is also part of the Mascarene Islands that include Mauritius and Reunion. Seychelles has the smallest population of any sovereign African State.

Maldives

The Maldives, with a population of 340,000 is the smallest country in Asia both in land area and population. It is also the lowest country on the planed with the average ground level being 1.5 meters above sea level. Maldives which covers an area that is 115 square miles also has the lowest point on planet Earth even though their greatest concern is the sinking of the Maldives.

Maldives is an island nation with 200 out of the about 2,000 Indian Ocean islands making up this country that gained independence in 1965. The Republic of Maldives is formed from a double chain of 26 atolls and is situated 435 miles south west of Sri Lanka. The entire number of atolls making up this country spread over close to 90,000 square kilometers which makes it the most dispersed country geographically in the world.

Malta

The island of Malta is located south of the Italian Island of Sicily and covers 122 square miles. It is a Southern European country with a population of close to 400,000 people making it among the worlds most densely populated countries in the world. It gained its independence in 1964 even though the British troops were not completely gone until 1979.

Malta is a world famous tourist resort country with its numerous historical monuments and recreational areas which include nine World heritage Sites nominated by UNESCO. Most prominent among them are the Megalithic Temples which are among the oldest free standing structures in the world.

Chapter Four

List of Physical Micronations

Micronations are entities that claim to be independent nations or states but are generally not recognized by international organizations or world governments. Many of them exist only on paper, in the minds of their creators as bright ideas or sometimes on the internet. The said micronations exist in numerous forms of government all dependent on what motivation was behind their creation. You will find them in republican, democratic, monarchic, and oligarchic or any other form of government you can think about.

The people who declare micronations are usually eccentric people or groups of people more often than not fail to secure widespread support and diplomatic recognition. There are even those micronations that have only one citizen whereas there are those with more inhabitants. When you consider that Talossa has had about 50 citizens who ever claimed citizenship at any time and the Hutt River Principality with over 20,000 citizens you therefore see the variance.

Many founders of micronations declare dominion over already existent land; most of this land is often isolated tiny islands and you will not be surprised to find some of it actually under water. Just like any ordinary nation, come micronations have their own decelerations of independence, written constitutions and even go ahead to seek for diplomatic recognition. Such even go as far as minting their own currencies and issuing passports to their residents.

The Federated Republics of A1

The federated Republics of A1 is a new micronation that was founded on 4th November 2010 following the conglomeration of the four protectorates that belonged to the former Most Glorious Republics of A1 which had been in existence since 2008. It has grown to be an extremely influential republic which originated from a classroom joke.

The original name for this micronation was originally simple A1 which was the name of the classroom. It was after a revolution that a decision was made to add the words "Most Glorious People's Republic of the beginning of 'A1'. It was the created by order of the chairman Pprit and it was hence carried over into the new republic in 2010.

The Aerican Empire

This micronation also goes by the name Aerica and is made of citizens with a distinct culture even though it is not recognized by other nations. The Aerican Empire began in Montreal, Canada in 1987and the name was formulated by a young boy of 5 years bordering on normalcy because it sounded like Eric.

The national flag of Aerica

The story goes on to say that as Eric continued to grow sillier Aerica itself continued to grow. It was beginning 1990 that Aerica had become an empire that would match the Star Trek Federation of Planets. The Empire's technology has continued to grow and so have the culture, relations, and power while at the same time eliminating the less realistic elements so as to make the empire a true nation.

The Aerican Empire did not have a good record of events happening therein before 1999 but after that year they founded an official news agency which keeps official records. As the empire progresses the events happening are recorded with greater accuracy.

The founders and proponents of the Aerican Empire will tell you that the location of their micronation is to be found on numerous locations both on earth and in outer space. Some specific locations include some land in Eastern Suburban Melbourne measuring 50 square kilometers. Also included are some private residencies in Montreal, New Zealand and some parts of the United States. Their land also includes some 2.9 km2 covering equatorial Mars as well as the Northern hemisphere of Pluto.

The Sovereign State of Aeterna Lucina

This was an Australian Micronation that was also referred to as the Sovereign Humanitarian Mission of Sate of Aeterna Lucina that existed from 1970 and died with its founder sometime in the 1990s. The founder called himself the "Supreme Lord" of Aeterna Lucina who was originally called Paul Robert Neuman.

The founder, a German Pensioner from northern Sydney made so many claims regarding him self. He claimed to have been given the title "Baron Neuman of Kara Bagh" from the exiled ex-king of Afghanistan and also claimed more than 850 honors among them Doctorates of Philosophy and Divinity and many other honors as well.

The empire that was named after the Roman goddess of childbirth originally occupied the land that belonged to Neuman at Byron bay. The state was to later relocate temporarily to Neuman Curl's residence before finally relocation to a14 km2 property near the town of Cooma, in New South Wales. It was at his residence that was known as Vitama that the capital city was t be found.

Soon thereafter the empire relocated to a 16 km2 secret location in Victoria and it is thought that it continues to operate and engage other similarly small corporate and judicial entities through the leadership of The Emira Aziza Akenzua, who is a Lucnian diplomat. It was not until 1990 when the state of Aeterna Lucina came to the public knowledge again when some of its senior citizens faced fraud charges. This included a Sydney Based businessman who faced fraud charges in relation to visa and land sale offences in the New South Wales judicial system.

Akhzivland

Akhzivland is a self declared independent state that is found in the pristine northern Mediterranean coastline of Israel. This was founded by a former seafarer Eli Avivi. He is said to have first set foot here in 1952 while visiting with his sister when he immediately fell in love with the land and dedicated to make his home there sometime in future. All that he found there were an empty coastline and an old Arab house that had been abandoned.

Akhzivland

It is bordered to the north by the hills of Lebanon and the mountains of Galilee to the east and the town of Acre to the south. The west opens up to the clear blue Mediterranean Sea. Born in Iran in 1930 to Jewish parents, the family moved to Tel Aviv in what was then British ruled Palestine. He was a naughty boy as he grew up and was arrested severally for trying to sabotage British trains by placing obstacles at time when there was a great upheaval in Palestine.

After joining the Jewish Underground Army in 1946 and the British leaving in 1947, he was part of the war between the Arabs and Jews that lead to the formation of State of Israel. After the war was over he worked on fishing boats in the Mediterranean and North Sea and later to Greenland and

Norway. Akhzivland State comprises a series of a grassy camp, some old buildings and large museum full of knick knacks and old interesting things.

Eli Avivi is the life president of the state which he runs almost on his own. He claims that he loved Israel and even fought for it and decided to make this his home forever. Since he didn't like the government he decided to make his won country and even made a passport for himself before declaring the place an independent country just like Israel did before him.

Eli Avivi stamping a visitor's passport

Eli Avivi once got arrested by the police and was put in jail for ten days before he was brought to a judge. The police charged him for creating a country without authority but luckily for him, the judge reminded the police that there was no such charge in existence anywhere in their penal code. The judge acquitted him and recommended that he be allowed to keep his own piece of land after all.

Mohammad Bahareth

The Crown Colonies of Antarctica

This is a free independent state in what was formerly known as the Kingdom of Mars. It covers a bug chunk of land in the Antarctica even though there are no established residencies in the territory. It is run by a government in absentia which operates from Kalamazoo, Michigan, in the United States of America. They are currently looking for willing residents and government officials after which the plan to relocate to the Antarctica.

The Kingdom was established in March 2001 covering several mountains in the Antarctica region. They also lay claim on the entire airspace and ground over all the territories they claim. However there is very little land over the Antarctica that is not covered by glaciers since it is all filled with Antarctic ice. They plan to use tunnel burrowing machines in order to get into the solid rock in the extinct volcanoes and mountains they have claimed.

Their plan is to install wind and solar power systems in the cities they are going to develop so as to heat heir homes. The plan is to develop wind farming techniques so as to tap the kattabatic winds that blow consistently from the South Pole. The founders believe will provide electricity all the year round which they believe will be good enough for the residents.

There is a plan to establish a supreme law for the Crown Colonies of the Antarctica which will be a flexible document that will be subject to changes over time depending on the experiences the residents will go through. In regard to citizenship interested people will be allowed to apply for the same through a particular email address with all members of the People of God Christian Churches automatically qualifying as naturalized citizens.

Antarcticland

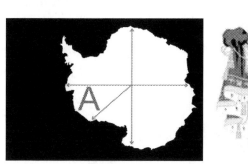 

The flag of Antarcticland The Coat of Arms

The Sovereign Order of the Knights of Antarcticland was established by Fabian Gottlieb Von Bellingshausen in 1821 because he was unhappy that the Tsar Alexander I did not give him sufficient recognition and credit for the discovery of the new continent. Even as Gottlieb continued to serve the Tsar he kept Antarcticland a secret after he was named an Admiral. In order to defend the territory of Antarcticland all the knights had to take an oath to total secrecy.

However, due to the difficulty in maintaining total control over the entire territory the Sovereign Order of the Knights of Antarcticland lost a considerable amount of their land during the 19th and 20th centuries. The order has been able to maintain a good amount of territory that extends from the South Pole to the 600 latitude and since no other sovereign state has claimed the territory it continues to belong to them.

There have been many economic and political changes in the world during the last century that have posed a real threat to the existence of Antarcticland to such an extent that the Grandmaster of the Order had had to release the knights from the vow to secrecy. The other threat to their territory is the effects of global warming.

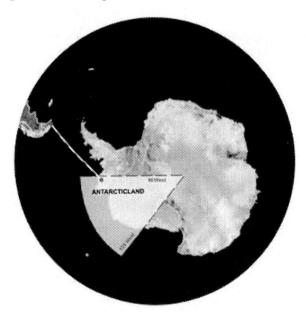

The location of Antarcticland

Kingdom of Apiya

The Kingdom of Apiya is a self proclaimed sovereign micronation located on the Balkan Peninsula in the European Continent. It is currently in its developmental stage by a community of like minded people intent on building a society which they intend to use as the basis of a new liberal society.

This is a new country project that invites all and sundry to join its ranks so as to have an input in making the dream come true. Citizenship is open to whosoever will and all you need to do is to click across an online application form and you will be done. The appeal is on for any ambitious and educated people to work on the concept and make it a reality.

The government system of Apiya is a constitutional Monarchy which is an improvement of the absolute monarchy that has been reigning. The idea of the governing style of Apiya is such that they want to create a modern monarchy in which the sovereign power dwells with the people.

The power in this country will create sufficient checks and balances between the three major arms of government: the executive, judiciary and the legislature. The driving motto of the Apiyan republic is liberty, equality, peace as well as the preservation of the environment.

According to the founders their greatest attraction will be the creation of the Apiyan language which is a constructed language being a conglomeration of Spanish, Macedonian,

Montenegrin, Italian and the now defunct Apiyan language. They base the cultural elements of cuisine, art, music on the Slavic cultures even though this may change because of the fact that many other people are joining the nation.

The Independent State of Aramoana

The Independent State of Aramonia is a brainchild of the Save Aramoana campaign that began in 1974 in opposition to the putting up of the Aramoana Aluminum smelter in New Zealand. A consortium of New Zealand based companies had proposed to set up an aluminum smelter at Aramoana in the late 1970s. This was going to lead to the destruction of the villages of Te Ngaru and Aramoana as well as threatening a local wildlife reserve.

When this information came to light the residents of the area duly announced their secession from New Zealand on 23rd December 190 and went further to establish a new border post as well as a travelling embassy. They also prepared citizenship certificates, passports as well as stamps. The resultant publicity is what they used to build up their national campaign in total opposition to the smelter.

The New Zealand government went ahead to approve the application of the consortium and they had plans to subsidize electricity costs so as to help the running of the smelter. However, due to fears by the rest of the population fearing for an upsurge in the cost of power; the Aramoanas received the local support in opposition and the government had to back down on its support of the project.

With such a development and the falling of the global aluminum prices finally led to the total withdrawal of the project. Eventually the members of the consortium began to disintegrate and for lack of a good capital venture they abandoned the project altogether. The reluctant effect was that the Independent State of Aramoana was reintegrated again with New Zealand.

The Kingdom of Araucania and Patagonia

The Kingdom of Araucania and Patagonia was established by the Mapuche Indians in 1860 by the territory now occupied by Chile and Argentina. The first King of the kingdom was a French lawyer, Arelie—Antoine de Tounens, who was however taken captive by Chilean soldiers in 1862 after which he was deported to France. He mounted about three expeditions to try and reclaim the throne he had lost by rallying the Mapuche against the Chileans until he died in 1878.

The royal house has therefore been living in exile in France for more than a century now and they still hold claim to the throne they lost. The current head of this royalty is known as Prince Philippe of Araucania who still maintains contact with Mapuche groups both in Europe and South America. He is also following up the case with United Nations Working Group on Indigenous People on behalf of the Mapuche who live in Argentina.

The Kingdom of Araucania and Patagonia may no longer exist as a state, which is a political apparatus but continues to exist as a nation of people with a common language, culture and history. The Mapuche people have preserved their unique cultural identity even in the face of the concerted effort to exterminate them. The use of force to incorporate them in a European or Western culture has done little to destroy their resolve to maintain the Mapuche culture, language, traditions, and language and land tenure.

The Empire of Atlantium

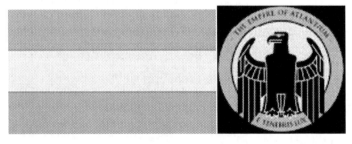

The Flag of Atlantium | The coat of Arms

The empire of Atlantium is a parallel sovereign state that is based in New South Wales, Australia. The concept of this micronation is that we are nearing the days of nations founded on fixed geographical locations. They are also against the concept of nations founded on major ethnic identities, cultural evolution as well as the development of electronic communication networks as the sign of the existence of a state.

The aim is to create a republic based on a people unified by common purposes and interests across the globe overtaking those traditional boundaries. The aim is to offer an alternative way of nationhood that will not be discriminatory due to the basis of where one was born, something one has no choice about whatsoever. The line of thought that created the Empire of Atlantium started as a local political statement by three teenagers in Sydney on the 27th November, 1981 and has continued to grow ever since. This is one of the largest not territorial states with citizens spread over some 90 countries.

The plan is built on a belief that it will soon become inevitable for the world to soon become one globally accepted social structure forming a political and economic union. It is going to be operating in a secular, liberal, social democratic republican monarchy. Citizenship to the Empire of Atlantium is open to all those who have a similar goal for them to consider joining.

The Empire of Austenasia

The founders of the Empire of Austenasia claim that it is a sovereign state that is completely separate from the United Kingdom since they fulfill all the requirements of a state in international law according to the Montevideo Convention. They have sent three different decelerations of independence to the British Government and so they believe that it is well aware of their existence. However the UK government does not recognize it a sovereign state.

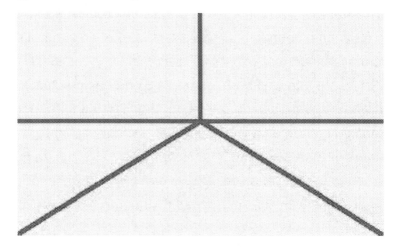

The flag of Austenasia

The government of Austenasia allows its subjects the privilege of dual citizenship; that means that they can also hold British citizenship and therefore they can also pay taxes to the British government if they area asked to. If anyone is a citizen of Austenasia alone they are not bound to pay British taxes, however, there are no people who fall in this category as yet.

People are allowed to visit their capital city, Wrythe with prior arrangements only. Zephyria is however out of bounds to tourists, reporters, journalists as well as TV crews. Citizenship is not open to everyone because one must first of all be a resident of Austenasia to qualify. The other way to become a citizen is to see combat under the Austenasia armed forces. The easier way to citizenship is however through becoming an honorary subject by applying online.

The empire is led by three teenagers: the Emperor Esmond III and Emperor Declan I who are the heads of state and prime minister who is the head of government. The Austenasia army is composed of about 22 soldiers who they claim will be ready to defend their country should a need arise especially if they will be battling another micronation. They also believe that should there be a full scale war with another large nation; the UK government will be ready to defend them since it recognizes them to be under her jurisdiction.

Their ministry of environment makes sure that the micronation is environmentally friendly by imposing an extra 20p in taxes for everyone who drives petrol or diesel powered motor vehicle. They claim to have taken an active part in the Erath Hour 2009 by turning off electricity for an hour alongside millions of other people in protest against energy consumption.

The founders claim that they have a tangible and practical goal and not authority hating rebels. They justify this by the fact that they own possessions and have a population of more than one person. The have a belief that eventually they will become recognized just like other micronations like the Principality of Sealand and Forvik.

Duchy of Bohemia

The Flag   The Coat of Arms

The Duchy of Bohemia is a self declared sovereign and independent micronation that operates as a government in exile with an embassy territorial enclave found within the territory of the United States of America. The claim sovereignty and they say they are not at all related to the Czech Republic or the Holy Roman Empire of the German Nation.

The current Czech government does not recognize the Duchy of Bohemia and neither does it recognize its claim of sovereignty. The founders claim that they own some small and well defined piece of land in the State of Nevada within the borders of USA. Their form of government is a Micronational monarchy. According to them they meet the criteria set forth in the 1933 Montevideo Convention of Rights and Duties of States, in spite of their small size.

The Dominion of British West Florida

The Dominion of British West Florida is a found in a former enclave of the British Empire and it lies between the Gulf of Mexico to the south and 32.28 degrees north. It is also in between Apalachicola and Chattahoochee rivers to the east as well as the mighty Mississippi River to its west.

The national Flag of the Dominion of British West Florida

The goal of the founders is to restore the Native Sovereignty of the people under the Crown and God. The aim of the Dominion within the Commonwealth nations is to make sure that West Florida becomes a Sovereign nation within the United Sates in relation to their Indian Tribal nations.

Since they believe that American Indians have been among the very well decorated War Veterans who ever served in the US Army they believe the residents of West Florida will serve then as well. They have a desire to be of the same status with other nations of the commonwealth realm such as New Zealand, Australia, Canada, Saint Kitts and Nevis, Antigua and Barbuda as well as the Bahamas.

The Dominion of West Florida advocates for the withdrawal of UK from the European Union as well as the revival of strong political links within he commonwealth nations. They want to hold fast to the ancient British tradition of having a strong Monarch as well as free subjects with a mutual respect for the rights, duties and privileges one to another. However their request has not been granted by her Majesty the Queen of the United Kingdom of Great Britain and Northern Ireland, and the Dominion of British West Florida and other Realms and Territories.

Bumbunga

The Province of Bumbunga refers to a secessionist Australian Micronation that was located on a farm at Bumbunga in Northeast of Adelaide during the 1970s and 1980s next to Snow Town and Lochiel. It was established by Alex Brackstone who was a British Immigrant from Australia who was previously a monkey trained, postmaster and uranium prospector.

When the Australian Labor party government was dismissed in November 1975 by the Governor—General John Kerr, who was the representative of the Queen, ardent British Monarchist Brackstone became alarmed at what he thought was a drift towards republicanism and wanted to ensure that part of Australia would still remain loyal to the British crown by whatever effort he would do.

It was under this set of circumstances that he declared his four hectare property to have seceded and become independent of Australia naming it the province of Bumbunga on March 29th 1976 and assigned himself the position of governor general. He went on to build a large scale model of Great Britain in his backyard using strawberry plants and used it as a tourist attraction.

He had intentions of using the facility to conduct weddings during which services there would be soil from appropriate counties would be sprinkled on the ground. This plan was however cut short when the Australian Customs Service prevented its implementation by seizing soil imported from UK by Brackstone. The whole enterprise thereafter came tumbling down when the strawberry plants dried out during a drought.

Bumbunga began to issue postage stamps in 1980 with British themes which proved very popular with collectors even though they could not be used for postage. In a little while there were significant changes to Australian investment laws and this had a great impact on Brackstone's business ventures which finally led to his abandoning it altogether in 1987.

After these events the Province of Bumbunga began a gradual downward slide and finally went under at around 1999. During this year Brackstone faced charges of possession of illegal firearms and was unsuccessful in trying to claim immunity due to the fact that he had designated himself governor general. He was subsequently repatriated to the United Kingdom.

The Conch Republic

The establishment of the Conch Republic happened when Florida Keys seceded from the United States of America on 23rd April, 1982 as a result of a Border Patrol Blockade on highway US1 at Florida City just outside Florida Keys. The citizens were isolated from the rest of the citizens of the mainland US since the blockade was in the main artery that connected them to the mainland. The residents were hence portrayed as non US citizens and had to show proof to the contrary so as to be allowed to drive through.

Since they considered this a totally un-American thing to do; the mayor of Key West Dennis Wardlow, together with several other 'Conchs' went to the Miami Federal Court to stop the blockade, but all was in vain. When they left the Federal court house they stood and announced to the world through the press that the following day at noon Florida Keys was going to secede from the Union.

The proclamation of secession was read the following day at noon at Mallory Square in Key West Florida by Mayor Wardrow who proclaimed that Conch Republic was now an independent nation separate from the United States. After about a minute of rebellion the mayor, who was now Prime Minister went to face the Admiral of the Navy Base at Key West surrendering to the Union forces. He even went on to demand for foreign aid and war relief of 1 billion dollars to help in rebuilding the nation following the long federal siege.

That marked the beginning of the Conch Republic where residents claim to belong to two nations, Conch Republic and the United States. In order to endorse their action about the validity of the recession, the 1994 Monroe County Commission passed by unanimous vote the County Resolution that recognized the actions of 23rd April 1982. They hold a celebration of their independence every year with a celebration that takes the whole week. The Secretary General has toured numerous Caribbean Nations with his diplomatic passport and is always received as an official of the Conch Republic.

The Gay & Lesbian Kingdom of the Coral Sea Islands

This micronation was established as a way of protest by a group of Australian gay rights activist based in Southeast Queensland. They simply wanted a real expression of sheer queer nationalism. The grouped laid claim of the Coral Sea Island territory on June 14th 2004 and declared it had seceded from Australia after sailing to the largest island in the group and raised their rainbow flag. Dale Parker was declared the emperor as Dale I.

This secession took place in response to a decision that was taken by the Australian Parliament to ban same sex marriages. The Australian group has however been embroiled in internal disputes and more secessions by various factions.

The Map of the area claimed by group

The claims of independence made by this group are not recognized by any state and there has never been any permanent residents settling in the Coral Sea Islands which remain uninhabited. The kingdom has claims to the effect that they began operating postal service on January 2006 even though there has not been any independent verification of these claims. However in July 2006 they issued their first postage stamps.

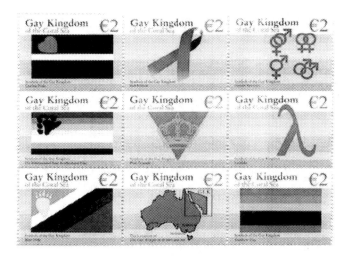

The set of 9 stamps belonging to the Kingdom

The Coral Sea Islands are spread over an area that spreads to total of more than 1 million square kilometers and was first administered as an overseas territory of England. There is no permanent fresh water and it is surprising that 90% of all the fish found n the kingdom are transgendorous; meaning that they change their sex at least once in their lifetime.

This is a constitutional monarchy which uses the British Common Law where applicable and it uses the Euro as its official currency. They have a national anthem written by Jerry Herman, who has been a long time public gay male and one of the longest survivors with AIDS in the world.

National Anthem

Mohammad Bahareth

I am what I am—by Gloria Gaynor.

I am what I am, I am my own special creation, so come take a look, Give me the hook or the ovation

It's my world that I want to have a little pride in, My world and it's not a place I have to hide in, Life's not worth a dam, Till you can say, hey world, I am what I am

I am what I am, I don't want praise, I don't want pity, I bang my own drum, some think its noise, I think it's pretty, and so what if I love each feather and each bangle, Why not try to see things from a different angle, Your life is a sham, Till you can shout out loud, I am what I am

I am what I am, and what I am needs no excuses, I deal my own deck, sometimes the ace, sometimes the deuces, there's one life and there's no return and no deposit

One life so it's time to open up your closet, Life's not worth a dam, Till you can say, hey world, I am what I am

Even though the kingdom has declared itself neutral militarily, it has a small army of gay activists located in all corners of the world who can be called to action at the shortest notice.

The Empire of Coromburg

The empire of Coromburg is a micronation that is looking for national statehood. It was established on December 11th, 2002 and became an empire on May 23rd, 2003. The founders claim that they are extremely serious and are not doing their exercise simply for fun even though they do not lay claim to any territory anywhere in the world that would have made them be recognized as a country.

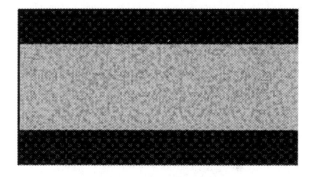

The national flag | The coat of arms

Currently the Empire is in the process of looking for land to set itself up either in East Tennessee or an island somewhere in the Caribbean. The Empire is currently looking for citizens and all you need to do is go to their website and visit the Ministry of Citizenship and Immigration. They have a national anthem that has borrowed the tune of "God Dave the Queen.

The National Anthem

"God on His righteous throne

Come down and guide us all

And make us strong.

Our Emperor is loved by all

Guiding our land along

Long reign to the Emperor

God save His soul."

The Kingdoms of Elgaland-Vargaland [KREV]

The Royal Kingdom of Elgaland-Vargaland was proclaimed in 1992 consisting of all border territories: geographical, mental as well as digital. It is supposedly the largest and most densely populated realm on earth and it incorporates all boundaries between all the nations of the entire world together with all digital territories and other states of existence. According to the founders, every time you travel somewhere else and every time you enter a different form such as when dreaming, you are actually visiting Elgaland-Vargaland

The Sovereign State of Forvik

The sovereign state of Forvik represents principles that give everyone the right to be truthful, transparent and accountability in governance. The kind of money it stands for is that which has real value as well as ethical banking practices. It also stands for making elected representatives servants rather than masters as you will find in many other nations. One of its other sore goals is doing away with thieves, liars as well as any form of tyrants who are found in government.

The Flag of the State of Forvik

It is the pursuit of these aims that leads to all activities in the formation of the Crown Dependency or offshore island state of

Forvik. Forvik is actually a part so Shetland and gives a small glimpse of what the entire Shetland could turn out to be. The main aim is to ask the UK government to give clear explanation as to where the authority of Shetland comes from.

The government has its own parliament known as The Ting which will be able to pass legislation that will back all its activities. It will be run under a direct democracy that will give sovereign power to the people and not politicians. Its guiding policy will be that any money that is generated will be spent entirely to help the residents reach their full potential. The other aim will be to protect and promote sustainable life that is going to be free from any corrupt government officials.

Since it will not recognize the sovereignty of the UK government over it will be doing for its citizen among other things that include: Low or Zero taxes for companies and individuals, issuing citizenships and passports as well as issuing its own currency—the gulde, a gold-based currency with real value. Other services will include issuing its own stamps, banking, company registrations, vehicle registration and licensing, ship and aircraft registration. Forvik claims all rights to the seas and seabed in its waters, duty-free goods in local shops and duty-free fuel.

The Ibrosian Commonwealth

This is a self proclaimed micronation with a sovereign state founded in the northern side of Great Britain that was founded on the 26th July 2001. It is based in the Estate of Amberly which also declared its independence from United Kingdom on the 27th January 1999.

The micronation is a project in classical liberalism as the state has evolved through a system of direct democracy that grew into a parliamentary representative democracy. The state has made claim of sovereign territory to some private property and the number of citizens is varied and not quite known.

The United Federation of Koronis

The Flag of the Koronis | The Coat of Arms

The United Federation of Koronis was established after the Koronis set of asteroids were given a new monarch on the 22nd April 2006. The federation has appropriated itself all asteroids even though it has based its activities on eight of the larger ones.

Since the asteroids are currently in a state that they cannot sustain life, the federation has some temporary offices on planet Earth for the sole purpose of conducting its activities and forming relationships. The form of government that has been established is a constitutional monarchy with members of a cabinet appointed each representing the eight larger bodies and it is they who are responsible for the running of government business.

The federation of the Koronis has had to device a system in order to facilitate business between the citizens and has even issued a currency.

One of the Asteroids that will be inhabited

It is important to take note that the cultural and economic exchanges that take a year on all the asteroids is set a timing that equals 4.9 years on earth. Therefore the ages of the citizens of Koronis are usually given in both Earth years as well as in Koronis years. The federation's headquarters is in the capital which is located in the entire asteroid of 243 Ida which is believed to have been explored by the Galileo spacecraft and there is sufficient information about it that is available.

The Sovereign Principality of Lavalon

The sovereign Principality of Lavalon is made up of like minded individuals who have for numerous reasons got tired and decided to secede from the current world powers. Those who are tired of the depressing and tiring reality and they decided the best way is to get out of it all can very well identify with Lavalonians.

The deceleration of the formation of Lavalon was signed on the 15th March 2003 and is based on a concept of nationhood not based on fate or accidental births, but by choice. This is a micronation where all citizens have freely chosen to belong and they are freely given the right to be citizens.

The people in charge of the Lavalonian government are presently the Sovereign Prince who serves with a democratically elected legislature that has the power to compel the Sovereign Prince to deliver. The system in its current form may appear to be absolutist and is power is all vested in the Sovereign Prince but with time things will no longer be the same. There is a lot of progress toward the formation of a democratic system of government.

Everyone who shares similar goals is invited to be a part of this wonderful process so that their bright ideas could also be incorporated in the formation of the new nation. Because this is going to be a small nation, every individual is going to wield considerable influence and this is a key motivation for those who would lave to see a different form of sovereignty.

The Dominion of Melchizedek

The Dominion of Melchizedek is an Ecclesiastical Sovereign Nation State which claims to hold on to traditions that go back in history to the Biblical Salem over which King Melchizedek was the Monarch. Since the people of Melchizedek greatly desired independence the leadership signed into law a formal constitution on 7th July 1991. This is when a government was formed that was based on ecclesiastical powers as well as democratic principles.

It was not until 26th November 1994 that the Dominion of Melchizedek got full acquisition and sovereignty of the Karitane Islands in the South Pacific. Once again on the 2th May 1999 they also got acquisition of the Taongi Islands in the North Pacific. Later in the year 2000 Melchizedek was once again in the news when Rotuma, which is to the North of Fiji signed a new constitution which granted Melchizedek all the rights and privileges such as those enjoyed by the Vatican in Rome

On 26th November 1994, the Dominion of Melchizedek acquired full ownership and sovereignty over the Karitane Islands in the South Pacific and on the 5th of May 1999 acquired sovereign rights over the Taongi Islands in the North Pacific from the island's Iroijlaplap. In the year 2000, Rotuma, which is north of Fiji, signed a constitution, wherein Melchizedek was granted all of the same rights and privileges enjoyed by the Vatican in Rome, and Melchizedek acquired sovereign rights over Solkope, one of the 7 islands surrounding Rotuma.

The formerly unclaimed 90-150 degrees West Antarctica was claimed by Melchizedek in 1990, and said claim was published in The City Paper in Washington DC in 1991.

The Principality of New Utopia

The future is here with us! That is the opportunity provided to all who will in the Principality of New Utopia, the micronation of the future. It is now possible to invest in a new adventure and free enterprise for all like minded individuals who have always sought higher aspirations. The vision of the Principality of New Utopia is to take higher calculated risks so that investors in the venture will reap higher and better results.

Flag of the Principality of New utopia

The founders of the Principality of New utopia are tired of being held captive by governments that more often than not stifle those with dreams and big visions who are actually the authors of the future. Business people with big dreams and whose business ventures are flexible enough to be mobile will have chance of a lifetime. For those not in any business, they will be welcome to become citizens of new utopia so as to make sure they have a safe haven for their future and that of their children.

The challenge faced by the Principality of New Utopia right now is getting international approval and recognition and thereafter get to interest thousands of like minded people. Those who are welcome are individuals who will want to use their brains in an extra ordinary way and using their courage and talent help to build the nation of the future. The location is perfect and there are enough incentives that will ensure the success of the venture.

An Artist's Impression of New Utopia

In order to make sure that the project keeps up with all emerging technological developments the board of governors will continually review the qualifications of those leading in numerous areas in the Principality of New Utopia. Those appointed will be given very fair compensation and such any people with skills; talents and expertise have such a great opportunity waiting for them.

Coins of New Utopia

The principality of New Utopia will be an opportunity for turning the world into a real global village where bright individuals will no longer be held captive by bankrupt governments.

This is why the Principality will be seeking to attract the most qualified people to become its citizens. This is a venture where entrepreneurship will be highly valued and every one who employs their skill and talent will receive a good return on investment.

Identification Card for residents of the principality of New Utopia

It will no longer be possible for those people with intellectual ambitions to become stifled where masses have a way of holding them down by popular vote. Those who are tired of leaders who lord it over them and who end up voting themselves big entitlements that are funded through obligatory taxes now have an opportunity to just turn things around.

Those who wish to get away from the current systems of government that are oppressive to the people who fund them through obligatory taxes have a chance to protest in a new way, they can vote with their feet and escape from that system for good. There is a chance to become a citizen of the coming new country known as New Utopia where business and adventure will go hand in hand.

Since there seems to be no other logical way to escape for the tyranny of the current government systems the only available alternative remains to move to a new country where like minded people will create a completely new way of doing things. This will help people escape from the current social parasitism and government intrusion into people's lives to a land of real personal freedom for all citizens.

The New Utopia will be known as 'The Venice of The Caribbean' and will come complete with canals and gondolas with waterfront restaurants and marinas and condos. All those achievers who want to become the real shakers and movers of the emerging future have a chance to become citizens of the Principality of New Utopia which will be the real gem of the ocean.

Chapter Five

The Top Ten Out of the Ordinary Micronations

If at anytime you ever wondered whether you could actually rule your own country, you will be amazed to discover that you are not alone. There a number of micronations that are actually claimed by one or more persons and they all strive for recognition by the rest of the countries. There are a number of these that have their strange histories which may include wars, triumph as well as independence.

Many existed only for a short time, were destroyed, annexed or even reclaimed from where they had seceded while others have defied the common way of doing things and continued to survive to date. Strangely, there are those that were one person's dream and they survived as long as that person was alive and died immediately the founder died.

There are also 'clever' people who establish micronations in order to either avoid paying taxes or even some con artists in order to get an avenue to defraud people. When you follow the histories of other micronation you will even get lost in the explanation as to why it was established in the first place.

In this section of our book we will look at ten of the most bizarre micronations which are best examples of strange reasons micronations are established. The list does not appear in any particular order but all in all they are all strange for different reasons altogether. A study through the list should show you that with determination then you can also establish a micronation and call it by your own name. Whether it survives or not is another story altogether; welcome to the world of weird micronations.

The Grand Duchy of Westarctica

The story of the Grand Duchy of Westarctica begins when the Antarctic treaty was signed and when Travis McHenry discovered that there was a piece of territory that no one had claimed he decided to claim the Marie Byrd Land. He decided to claim the land as an individual and then established a country on the said land.

Location map of Westarctica

Travis McHenry sent letters to the governments of France, Russia, Norway, Argentina, Chile, Australia, United Kingdom and the United States to inform them of the new development and as expected they all ignored his letters. It was in 2004 that McHenry decided to change the name of his new country and called it The Grand Duchy of Westarctica.

The following year he went on to lay claim on the Balleny Islands as well as the Peter I Islands but they had already been claimed by New Zealand and Norway Respectively. The head of state has been Jon—Lawrence Langer, the Duke of Moulton—Berlin and he has requested Westarcticans and all their allies to come to his help and develop the micronation into reality.

The national Flag of Westarctica

He was however removed from power on 3rd June 2010 following a list of complaints and disputes in running of the micronation. McHenry has gone on to replace the Grand Duchy with the Protectorate of Westarctica. Several reforms are going on and the micronation has adopted anew flag and joined the Antarctic Micronation Union. Not much is known about the intentions of the founder of this micronation and the most that has ever come out of it a re a few coins and stamps as well as a free email service for all citizens.

Coins from the Grand Duchy of Westarctica

Pitcairn Island

Of the entire list of micronation none has a more moving story than that of the Island of Pitcairn. It all begins with a mutiny aboard 'The Bounty' which was anchored in what is now referred to as Bounty Bay. The mutineers ransacked the ship of all its precious cargo and took it all up the 'Hill of Difficulty' to a grassy platform there.

Pitcairn Island

Since they feared any retribution should 'The Bounty' be sighted bay any European vessel, the mutineers ran it ashore and set it on fire.

The founder and first leader of the settlement here was Fletcher Christian who was the leader of the mutiny. With his cheerfulness and energy he obviously became the leader who was loved and cheered by his fellow even though he died shortly after settling on Pitcairn.

When they landed here the mutineers constructed some leaf shelters at the location of the village called Adamstown but in a little while there were wrangles that lead to friction with the eventual result being murders. The treated the Tahitians like slaves and this lead to a revolt that lead to the deaths of a number of them. Only Young, Adams, Quintal and McCoy were still remaining by 1794 to lead the households of ten women and several children.

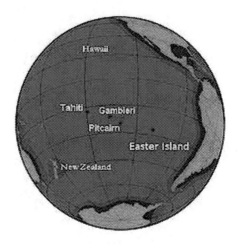

Location maps of Pitcairn

They lived peacefully for the next four years even though there were occasional outbreaks by the women who some of the time attempted to leave the tiny island but in vain. They spent their time building houses, fencing and cultivating patches of land as well as trying to trap birds and hogs for their daily food.

The Flag of Pitcairn

When the initial friction was over the men and women reconciled their lives to each other and all was in harmony until

McCoy decided to brew a potent spirit from the roots a local plant. By 1799 John Adams was the sole male survivor of the party that had landed here ten years earlier.

The island is not officially considered a nation but referred to as an unincorporated territory. It runs as a democracy with mayor of the town considered as its leader and that would qualify it as the smallest democracy in the world.

The Republic Molossia

The Republic of Molosia was established in 1977 as a school project by Kevin Baugh who is also the president of the republic. It has been described as a mock dictatorship based in northern Nevada but the ruler describes it as a hobby. The founder loves to describe his country as an enclave surrounded by the United States of America that has a population of three people.

The Coat of Arms
The President

The country has a constitution and a national assembly and when it comes to the law, the president claims that martial law is in operation. The reason he gives for that is the ever present threat from foreign states and in particular the United States.

This micronation has claims on some territory in Pennsylvania as well as Northern California and the most recent claim it has made has been on the 'Neptune Deep' which is the deepest trench in the Pacific Ocean as well as the province of 'Vesperia' which is located on the planet Venus.

The president of the republic, Kevin Baugh has also decreed a ban on several items which include smoking, incandescent light bulbs as well as firearms. Other outrageous bans by the president include walruses, catfish, onions or anything that comes from Texas.

Many people however consider the place a tourist trap because you can be given a country wide tour by the president himself and this last close to one hour. You will however be required to present your passport at the gate so as to be granted a visa.

Freetown Christiania

Freetown Christiania may not be your everyday micronation but is considered as a self governing entity that has a small resident population. It was founded way back in 1971 and established on an abandoned military base in Copenhagen, Denmark. The founders were basically freethinkers and hippies whose real intention was to build a 'free' society.

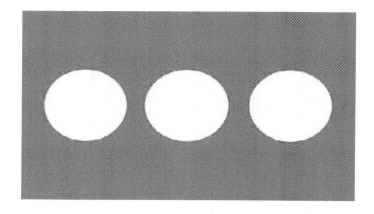

There are many different world views regarding Freetown Christiania with some people feeling it is the world's pioneer fully functioning anarchistic society while others consider it a haven for drug dealers and squatters. For some people this is a safe quiet town where there is so much freedom whereas others consider it a den for all manner of criminals where there are more rapes, muggings and murder than you could care to think about.

Even though no official numbers in terms if crime exists the area has become a real anarchist state which is so different from what the founders had in mind. The town's area is less than a kilometer square and the residents dutifully pay their rates and taxes to Copenhagen even though they claim the town has its own independent laws and public services.

Among the things that are forbidden include firearms, hardcore drugs, cars and cameras but it is unclear how these can be enforced since the town does not have a police force. The major attraction in this town is what is referred to as 'Pusher Street' because drugs such as marijuana can be bought freely in an open air market.

With this kind of reputation of free open air drug dealing which is illegal in the rest of Denmark, Freetown Christiania happens to be home for a large number of Danish authors, artists as well as theatre groups. It appears to be the best living example on how anarchy can thrive in a system of government.

The Nation of Celestial Space

This would basically be the winner if the micronation laid claim on all the territory it claims to be its own. The Nation of Celestial Space which was founded in the 1st January 1949 by James Thomas Mangan claims the entire universe, save for the earth to be previouly unclaimed territory.

The flag of the Nation of Celestial Space and the national seal

This claim may be as weird as they come but it did not prevent James Thomas mangan from minting coins, postage stamps and bills for his 'new nation'. He even went further to write letters of complaints when the United States and Russia began to fly high altitude aircraft claiming that the flights were an infringment of his terrtorial space without permission.

There have been several other people who have tried to establish micronations before the signing of the Outer Space Treaty of 1967 which prohibited laying claim to ouer space by anyone or any nation. There were other people before him that included the 'other world nation' which claimed all th eother planets of the solar system as well as the 'Celestial Solar Kingdom' which laid claim on the entire surface of the sun

Rose Island

An Italian architect and real—estate investor Giorgio Rosa decided to construct a 400 square meter platform in 1968 in the Adriatic Sea some 7 miles off the town of Rimini, in Italy. This was initially meant to be a tourist spot which would host a souvenir shop, fishing pier and a radios station.

The platform was supported by nine pylons and it was also furnished with several commercial outlets: restaurant, bar, night club and a post office. As soon as it was opened his mind got the better side of him and he declared the platform a sovereign micronation and renamed it the Republic of Rose Island. Rosa declared its independence on 24th June 1968 and he declared himself the president. The government went on to issue some stamps even though they never issued any coins or banknotes.

The Italian government got worried and thought this was a scheme in order to avoid paying taxes after earning money from tourism. Event though it was not known whether this was the real motivation behind Rosa's declaration of independence the government reacted swiftly and decisively. A group of four carabinieri and tax inspectors assumed control of the platform after evicting Rosa and his employees.

The platform's council wrote a protest note to the Italian government regarding violation of their sovereignty and injury to their tourism industry but it was ignored. Soon thereafter the Italian navy came in and completely destroyed the platform using explosives. However, Rosa never gave up and decided to print the macronations postage stamps issuing them from his 'Government in Exile'.

Conch Republic

The Conch Republic is the best example of a micronation that was established as a protest even though others consider it a comedy. When the US Border Patrol decided to mount a check point between the mainland and Florida Keys the residents were not excited. The purpose for the check point was to check an influx of illegal immigrants from Cuba and other Caribbean islands but it unfortunately caused a gridlock on the only highway bridge become an impediment to shipping and tourism.

After a failure in dialogue mayor Dennis Wardlow declared himself prime minister of the Republic of Conch on 30th April 1982. They even declared a state of war with the United States during the secession by breaking a stale loaf of Cuban bread over a nearby naval officer. He thereafter quickly surrendered and asked the US government for a one billion dollar aid to assist in post war reconstruction.

Even though the secession was never taken seriously by anybody else the Florida Keys still refer to themselves as the

Conch Republic but finally the protest succeeded in persuading Border Patrol to remove the check point. In 1994 the people of Conch Republic came together to re-open a national park that had been closed by the United States earlier. Their national Motto is "We Seceded Where Others Failed".

On the 20th September 1995 the 478th public affairs battalion of the USA Army Reserve planned to conduct a training exercise that simulated a foreign island invasion and the chose to land on Key West. However there was no notification by the 478th battalion to officials of Key West.

This provided a good opportunity for the prime minister of Conch Republic to get the publicity he had always longed for. He mobilized the entire island for a full scale war with the United States in protest to the Department of Defense planning an exercise without consulting the officials of Key West. Their form of defense involved firing water cannons from fireboats and hitting people with stale Cuban bread. The 487th battalion apologized the following day and thereafter submitted to a surrender ceremony on the 22nd of September.

Once again in December 1995 there was another protest where the Conch Republic the Dry Tortugas National Park so as to reopen it. The local residents were inspired by the efforts of the Smithsonian Institution to keep museums open by private donations and they tried to raise the money to keep the park running. However, there was no one to hand over the money that had been raided to in order to reopen the park.

The officials tried to enter the monument but they were cited and the citation was contested in a court case the following year. However the case, The United States of America V. Peter Anderson was dropped as soon as it was filed. The Conch Republic has opened consulate offices in France and Finland

The government of the Conch Republic offers regular and diplomatic passports as well as offering citizenship to anyone who is willing regardless of where they reside. However, the United States or any other foreign state does not recognize these as valid travel documents. The Conch Republic itself agrees that the passports are mere souvenirs even though some residents believe they can be used as valid travel documents.

Republic of Minerva

Minerva was discovered way back in 1852 by a group of American whalers but it was not until 1942 that there was any real occupation. This was when the US military forces occupied the atolls and islands during the Second World War. In 1971 barges came from Australia loaded with sand and brought the reef to above the water and allowed for the construction for a small tower and flag.

Landing in Minerva Reef

The Republic of Minerva was the brainchild of a Nevada businessman Michael Oliver who had in the early 1970s announced his intentions to reclaim some land from the South Pacific Ocean in order to establish a libertarian inspired city—state that could sustain close to 30,000 people.

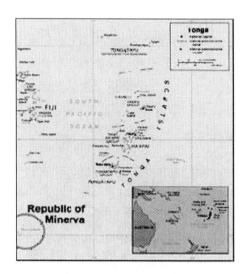

He chose a site that was 400 miles south of Fiji and 260 miles west of Tonga which was the location of previously unclaimed underwater reefs. The construction began in 1971 and Minerva declared itself an independent state on 19th January 1972. Letters were issued to neighboring countries and in February 1972, Morris C. Davis was elected the provisional president of the Republic of Minerva.

Flag of Minerva

Unfortunately the declaration of independence was greeted with a lot of suspicion by many countries in the neighborhood. The neighboring countries held a conference of states that was attended by Australia, New Zealand, Fiji, Tonga, Western Samoa, Nauru and Cook Island on the 24th February 1972 where Tonga made claim over the Minerva Reefs. The Tongan government reacted to this unwelcome threat by sending a naval gunboat, a convict work detail and a rowboat populated by the king and a brass band to Minerva. On 21st June 1972 the atoll was annexed by Tonga Kingdom and the Minerva flag hauled down.

Minerva Reefs

The idea behind the creation of Minerva was to have a truly libertarian utopia where residents would pay no taxes, subsidies or welfare. The high hopes that were held by the citizens of the tiny island were dashed before they could bear fruit. They thought they could have attracted fishermen, tourist and even industry thereafter after adding more sand to the island in order to make it habitable.

When the reefs were claimed by the Kingdom of Tonga, all that Oliver was left with was to fire the president in order to cut his losses. Many years later president Davis tried to return with an expedition of American settlers with an aim of reoccupying the reefs but the Tongan Army kicked then out again. The most recent expedition to this artificial island discovered that more or less the reefs had been reclaimed by the sea.

Principality of Sealand

This could as well be among the weirdest of all the
micronations; the Principality of Sealand is located on former
World War II gun platform, Maunsell Sea Fort at the HM
Forth Roughs in the North Sea approximately six miles off the
coast of Suffolk, England. However, the principality is not at
all recognized as a sovereign state by any of United Nations
member states. Fort Roughs was placed in a British shipping
lane so as to fend off German mine laying aircraft. As the
Second World War raged the 550 square meter platform hosted
107 UK sailors and observation towers.

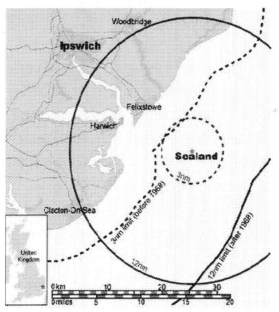

Major Paddy Roy Bates, a British subject and pirate radio
broadcaster occupied the fort on 2nd September 1967 after
ejecting competing pirate broadcasters with the intentions
to broadcast his pirate Radio Essex from the platform. The

platform itself existed in international waters and therefore there little the British government could do about pirate broadcast.

Sometime later Bates' son was fired a rifle at a crew that was repairing a buoy near the platform and this led to his arrest on charges of firearms violations since they were still consider British Citizens. Since the platform was some three miles off UK's territorial waters Bates was acquitted and this gave him an opportunity to declare the platform 'The Principality of Sealand. He went on to write a national anthem, started a currency and even issued stamps, stating that the court gave him the right to declare the open sea platform a sovereign nation.

However, while Bates was away sometime in 1978, the Prime Minister of Sealand, Professor Alexander G. Achenbach and several German and Dutch Citizens forcibly took over the Roughs Tower and held Bates' son captive only to release him several days later in the Netherlands.

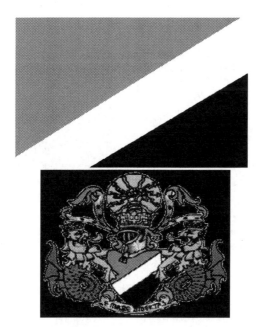

The flag of Sealand | The Coat of arms

Bates decided to enlist some armed resistance and retook the fort after a helicopter assault and held the invaders captive with the claim that they were prisoners of war. Most of those who had participated in the invasion were repatriated at the end of the war apart from Achenbach, a German lawyer who held a Sealand passport was charged with treason against Sealand and was ordered to pay a fine of $35,000.

The Netherlands and Germany governments petitioned the British government for his release but the UK disavowed all responsibility. It is after this that Germany decided to send a diplomat from its London embassy to Rough Tower to seek the release of Achenbach. After weeks of negotiations Roy Bates relented and went on to claim that the visit by the German diplomat constituted recognition of the Principality of Sealand by Germany.

After his release Achenbach went on to establish a government in exile in Germany in opposition to the one of Roy Bates and assumed the position of "The Chairman of the Privy Council."

When he became so ill in 1998 he handed over the position to Johannes Seiger who continues to hold it and still claims to be the legitimate leader of Sealand.

Principality of Hutt River

The Hutt River Principality is a seventy five square kilometer self declared independent nation-state in an enclave that is located some 595 kilometers north of Perth, Australia. It was established by a farmer named Leonard George Casley on 21st April 1970 when he and his associates announced their secession from the Western Australian State and the commonwealth of Australia.

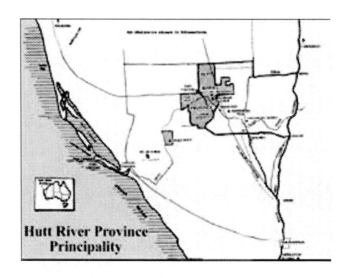

Location map of Hutt River Province

The Casley family had been involved in a tussle with the Western Australian government about the reduction of wheat quotas. They feared that the new quotas would render their farming business fiscally unviable if they were to be imposed. The legislation did not seem to allow any future revision of those quotas and also denied any compensation to affected parties. In response to this Leonard Casley decided it was time to form a government of self preservation that would have authority of their farmlands.

Casley went on to send formal notifications of secession to the state and federal officials and he got duly elected as the administrator of the new Hutt River Province. Soon thereafter he assumed the position of prince becoming His Royal Highness Leonard I with a population of 12 people in the new state.

The Flag of Hutt River Province

The announcement gained quick public attention and soon bus loads of tourists were visiting to see the new nation's capital. The hamlet of Nain soon boasted a secession monument, government buildings, a multidenominational chapel as well as a post office that would soon thereafter release postage stamps. Banknotes and coins followed suit in quick succession and this lead to the principality having a sound economic footing.

In a little while the price of Hutt province was issuing passports and visas while appointing ambassadors to represent its interests around the world. The Principality was soon crowded with all manner of regalia, Orders of Knighthood that would bedeck many friends, supporters and family.

The Coat of arms

None of these activities were recognized by the Australian government and indeed some agencies questioned its very existence. This led them to do all they could to make life extremely difficult for the new prince and his family. The Australian government threatened to demolish Nain which had apparently been constructed without any authority while the Australian Postmaster general placed an embargo on the entire Principality's mail to Australia instead rerouting it to Canada.

Any unpleasant physical confrontation was avoided even when the Prince did an act of provocation by declaring war on Australia leading to a confrontation that lasted a few days even though there was no action from any of the parties involved.

There are over 18,000 people worldwide who claim to be citizens of the Principality of Hutt River Province which has gone on to mark the 40th anniversary celebrations since it was founded. The determination of Leonard Casley has transcended his own achievement and obtained a degree of immortality and has been subject of an exhibition in the Australian National Museum in Canberra.

There have been futile attempts to establish a radio station and an air force but surprisingly the landlocked nation has managed to establish a Royal Navy using a fleet of privately owned Yachts. The Hutt River province decided to declare itself a Kingdom in the late 1980s but this was short lived and it reverted to its original status of a principality.

Passport issued by the Hutt River Principality

Even after existing for forty years and calling itself a sovereign state the Principality of Hutt River Province has never been recognized by the Commonwealth of Australia or any other state or international organization. The Principality continues to issue passports, stamps and coins that bear the portrait of the former American president Bill Clinton.

The secession Monument in the Capital—Nain

It claims to have a population of close to 18,000 people who live abroad and anyone who wants to become a citizen can apply and receive it at a small fee. Its military consists mainly of Casley's children and grand children. Even though the Australian government does not recognize the Hutt River Province as a real country, it regards it as a tourist attraction with an old man selling souvenirs to tourists. Many tours to the Australian Wilderness nowadays include a stopover at Hutt

River Province in what has been billed "The Second Biggest nation on the Continent."

Chapter Six

The Most Famous Micro Nations

Most people who have never heard about micronation always think the smallest nations are such like Monaco, Andorra, Luxembourg and etc. the truth of the matter however is that those are huge countries when compared to some of the smallest micronations which are however extremely famous.

Whereas some of these mini-states occupy areas as small as an acre of land, there are those that are even smaller than your mind can imagine. As usual they are almost always never recognized by their legitimate counterparts but this has not stopped people's fascination with establishing them at the slightest opportunity. This is why any list of micronations can never claim to be conclusive because you never know when another one is going to be established.

Ladonia

If you are looking for a really strange micronation then you need to consider Ladonia, which is a mini-state made of driftwood and nails. It is actually a nine storey wooden fortress found hidden at the southwest corner of Sweden. The micronation is made up of two work of art designed by Professor Lars Vilks.

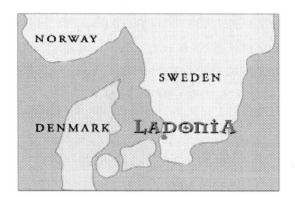

One is known as Nimis, which is a maze made from over 70 tons of driftwood and nails and the other one is Arx which is a stone and concrete sculpture that resembles a melting sandcastle. It may sound strange but the very nature of Ladonia is actually uninhabitable but that did not stop close to 3,000 Pakistanis from applying for immigrant status only to realize later what the micronation really looks like.

Nimis, in Ladonia is a simple series of wooden sculptures that is found along the coastline in the Kullaberg Nature Reserve in the northern part of Skane County in Sweden. They are such a massive collection of driftwood whose construction began in 1980 and their very existence has been a subject to legal disputes between the artist and the Swedish government. It is such a popular tourist attraction event though the authorities simply want to pull it down.

Nimis
The Arx

There are no signposts leading to Nimis and neither is it to be found in any official map because its existence is not sanctioned by the government. Vilks has somehow managed to dodge the government's interference in his project by selling the Nimis to another artist known as Cristo and thereafter declaring it an independent sate in 1996.

The micronation of Ladonia claims to be home to more than 15,000 citizens who live in exile since they are all supposed to nomads. There is even a national flag and a national anthem called "Ladonia for thee I fling." It was written by the renowned Walter Ehresman who is the country's Minister of Dubious Anthems.

The micronations Flag

Most of those citizens happen to be fellow artists who are main supporters of his cause. They claim to have a local currency known as the Ortug and a national language which is some form of phrased Latin. The micronation continues to try and impress Sweden which has never recognized it as a legitimate nation.

The Kingdom of Redonda

The Kingdom of Redonda is a tiny micronation in a rocky outcrop found between the islands of Nevis and Montserrat in the Caribbean Sea. The island, which is currently a dependency of the country of Antigua and Barbuda, is actually still uninhabited.

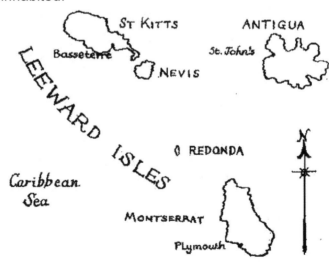

Location map of the Kingdom of Redonda

Redonda itself is a name borrowed from a micronation which appears to have existed as an independent kingdom sometime in the 19th century. The title to this kingdom is still contested to this very day. The kingdom is supposedly associated with a number of aristocratic members who keep on exchanging the title freely and whoever is supreme at any one moment is aptly called the king. There are therefore a number of numerous individual all who claim to be the King of Redonda.

The idea of making it a kingdom is supposed to have originated with Matthew Phipps Shiell who lived between 1865 and 1947 and was a prolific author or fantasy fiction. He went on to claim that his father who lived in a nearby Montserrat island was the rightful legal king of the island of Redonda.

This he must have done so that he could rightfully declare himself the heir to the throne. He published promotional leaflets for his books that continued to propagate this idea. After Matthew Phipps died in 1947, John Gawsworth took over the claim to the throne as King of Redonda King Juan I and thereafter after the death of Gawsworth, Arthur John Roberts descended the throne as King Juan II.

The Redonda Flag

As such, the story of the Kingdom of Redonda has gone on being a mixture of fact and fiction with claim over an uninhabited rocky outcrop till now. Most people who have served as king have never lived there and the island is simply desolate. Legend has it that Sheill once wrote to Queen Victoria of England asking for recognition to which the Queen is said to have replied that she was willing so long as he never rebelled against the crown.

Postage Stamps from the Kingdom of Redonda

The crown has been passed over 100 citizens of Redonda and at any one time there are likely to be about three claimants in waiting for the throne. The most famous of them appears to be a Spanish author Javier Marias who has given out ceremonial titles in the Kingdom of Redonda to a number of artists among them being Ray Bradbury, Alice Munro and Francis Ford Coppola.

Set of nine coins from Kingdom of Redonda

Global Country of World Peace

The founder of the global country of world peace is the renowned Maharishu Mahesh Yogi who is known to have grown up with the Beatles. He has tried all he can to establish a really global micronation. He has been known to offer over one billion dollars to the tiny and impoverished nations of the world and expecting to get a portion of their sovereignty. The nation has a prime minister named Bevan Morris and is based in Iowa.

Maharishu Mahesh Yogi

The Global Country of World Peacewas founder on 7th October 2007 and was described as a country without borders for all the peace loving people of the world. The structure of the nation is an absolute monarchy with Maharaja Adhiraj Rajaraam as the current Sovereign Ruler. It was incorporated in the state of Iowa on 15th October, 2002 as a non profit organization. The headquarters is in Maharishi Vedic City, Iowa. It is said to be building capitals in Netherlands, Iowa, Kansas, Manhattan, West Virginia and India.

This is the official currency of this unofficial microstate. It is called the Raam.

It is said that the official currency of the country, the Raam has been used and accepted in Iowa as well as in Netherlands where it is said to be equivalent to 10 Euros per Raam. It is also called the peace currency and it is expected that it will be used globally.

Maharishi is said to have inaugurated the program for the establishment of a global administration in July 1996 through natural law and the following year, January 12th 1997 he inaugurated the 'year of global administration. This established a global administration for the entire world with twelve time zone capitals so as to take full advantage of the administration of natural law that is centered in the life giving sun.

The life giving power of the sun is said to be what influences the earth to change from month to month and the creation of new seasons while constantly maintaining the evolutionary nature that is the natural law of life all over the universe. This is what is going to provide the philosophy of administration that will offer new programs and principles that will endow all nations with wealth through a natural law that will nourish all countries.

The focus of the natural law in the Global Country of Peace will be on all areas of administration but the primary focus will be to apply the natural law in areas such as health and education. The goal is that there will be total knowledge and enlightenment as well as perfect health for every one in the world. This is what will thereafter spontaneously make the administration of justice free from all challenges which are usually due to lack of good health and proper education.

The inspiration of Maharishau Mahesh Yogi

Once Maharishi's Global Administration is established
through the use of natural law and its administration through
national law in all countries in the world, countries will begin
to experience fewer problems in their administration and
governments that adopt this program will rise the dignity of
sovereignty they have always sought, self sufficiency as well as
invincibility.

The training of these global administrators is already taking
place in the Maharishi Universities of Management as well as
the Maharishi Vedic Universities so as to uplift government

administration through natural law. This training will enable leaders to be at par with the perfect administration of the government of nature through natural law. When this is accomplished everyone will rise above the level of problems and every government will gain the ability to fulfill its role for its entire population.

Flag of the Global Country of World Peace

The philosophy of the Global Government of world peace can be summarized as follows:

1. World peace has been the long-sought goal of many generations. The Transcendental Meditation Programme provides an effective solution to the problem of world peace.

2. A peaceful world means a world of peaceful individuals, just as a green forest means a large number of individual trees that are green. The individual is the basic unit of society. A peaceful

individual is the unit of a peaceful world. We can break the big problem of world peace into small problems and solve it on the level of the very nature of the individual. Bring peace to all individuals, and the problem of world peace is solved.

3. World peace can be a practical reality when the individuals of every nation are healthy, happy, and harmonious within themselves, and spread this nourishing influence in their relationships with others. Until this happens, conflicts are inevitable.

4. Happiness is the basis of peace. Unless one is happy, any sense of peace one has will be constantly disturbed. A lasting state of happiness cannot be gained by anything in the outer, ever-changing field of life. The mind's great thirst for lasting happiness can only be satisfied by contacting the field of infinite happiness, energy, and intelligenceÑthe source of thought deep within the mind. Allowing the mind to experience its more quiet levels naturally structures a permanent state of happiness, harmony, and peace.

5. World peace is within the reach of every nation when happiness is within the reach of the citizens of the nation. As soon as the individuals of every nation begin to live in harmony and peace, world peace will be automatic and permanent.

6. Every individual influences his surroundings through every thought, word, and action. These influences are either life-supporting or life-damaging. When people are happy,

productive, and at peace within themselves, their surroundings reflect their state of well-being, and peace is a natural result. When people are unhappy, restless, and tense, the atmosphere becomes saturated with these life-damaging influences and peace is disrupted. National and international conflicts are caused by the collective effect of tensions that individuals generate in their environment. As long as individuals continue to grow in stress and tension, world peace can only remain an abstract and fragile idea.

7. Transcendental Meditation dissolves stress within the individual by providing deep rest. At the same time the individual is strengthened, so he accumulates less stress and fatigue in daily activity.

8. Any individual who is free from stress naturally generates happiness and harmony in his surroundings, and thereby contributes his share for world peace.

9. The nature of life is to progress. Change is a constant phenomenon in creation because progress through change is the nature of life. Peace is the basis of progress, but progress maintains peace. To be progressive, one must be more creative day by day.

Lundy

The island of Lundy is known to be the world's oldest and may be the most legitimate of all micronations in the world. It has been occupied from the Neolithic age and is located in the Bristol Channel and only coming under very strict control of England in the last about 40 years.

Marisco's Castle on Lundy Island

It began as a base for Norse Sea raiders and was first owned by the Knights Templar during the 12th Century but was taken over during the 13th century by William De Marisco who established a stronghold the reigned over it as a sovereign. The Mariscos were actually a 13th century pirate or mafia clan and they ruled until one would be assassin of King Henry III confessed to being one of their agents.

When this information came to light King Henry III sent troops to run over the island, hang and thereafter build a castle to establish his rule. However, because this island at the Bristol Channel was the perfect pirate base England did not hang onto it for as long as they had expected.

The island was once again conquered in the 1600s by the Barbary Pirates and they flew the Ottoman flag over it. They later used it as a holding pen for slaves they would capture from the Irish and English coasts and they would later ship them back to Algeria where they most probably had come from.

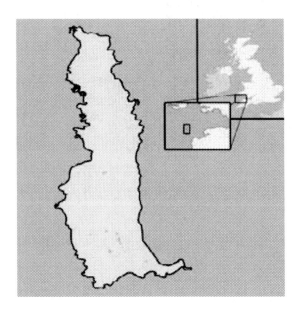

During the 18th century Lundy had another great period to its history when it was property of the Sherriff of Devon who was also a one time MP Thomas Benson. He had gotten into an agreement with the government that he would ship convicts to the colony of Virginia, but being a sky man, he would keep all of them as slaves on his own island.

For about a century the island was also owned by the Haven family and as usual they kept on to the tradition of rejecting control from the mainland. This went on until 1924 when a man called martin Coles Harmon proclaimed himself king and he actually started minting coins even though he never declared total independence.

The island went up for sale later when his son died and it later ended up in the hands of the Landmark Trust. The island is currently home to about 30 residents and there are about 20,000 tourists who visit it annually.

Lighthouse on Lundy Island

Other World Kingdom

The Other World Kingdom is a large commercial resort that is also micronation that is based in a 16th century chateau in the Czech Republic. It is also described as the 'private state of supreme women'. This micronation exists for only one reason, and that is to get as many male creatures as they possibly can under the total rule of supreme women and on as much territory as is practically possible.

The founders of the Other World Kingdom have intentions of finally establishing an Absolute Matriarchy where women will rein the world supreme. It should be noted that this micronation is not a sex resort. The forms of domination they intend to employ appear to be extremely severe with very little if any seductive qualities whatsoever.

It is also their policy that there will be no sexuality or any sexual contact in the Other World Kingdom if the behavior seen on their videos is anything to go by.

They have a strong desire to get male creatures that they can actually lean on a leash, poop on and even spend the entire day whipping and treat them at the lowest level possible. That appears to be among the weirdest of all micronations in existence today. For anyone to become a citizen and join the already 34 noble ladies who belong there already, you need to have at least one male slave so as to qualify.

The Principality of Outer Baldonia

Size: .00625 of a square mile

The Principality of Outer Baldonia is a micronation that was established in 1948 by a notorious eccentric known as Russell Arundel. They stumbled upon an island while sports fishing with a group of friends in Canada off the coast of Nova Scotia.

Flag of principality of Outer Baldonia

He loved the island and bought the four acre Outer Bald Tusket for $750, built a small fishing lodge and would go there regularly especially on drinking sprees with his friends. It was during one late night drinking sessions that Arundel and his friends decided to draft a constitution that stipulated that fishing and drinking were time honored pastimes in the island.

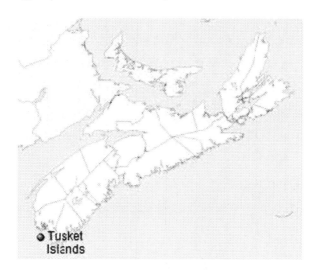

Location Map for The Principality of Outer Baldonia

They declared independence and then called it the Principality of Outer Baldonia and went on to dole out government titles among themselves. Any group member who caught a tuna and paid a prescribed fee was given the title prince and then they went forward to develop a currency. They later released a State Charter that stated taxes and women were banned from the island, and that its main export was empty beer bottles.

Baldonia would have remained a practical joke between Arundel and his friends but he went further and listed his office number in Washington DC making it the embassy of the

Principality. In a little while his imaginary country was getting invited to numerous state functions and it actually got invited to join the United Nations by mistake.

The micronation that Arundel had established went on to become more famous to an extent that a soviet newspaper wrote about it criticizing it. The response that Baldonia wrote in response was a declaration of war. The Baldonian Navy, which was made up of local fishing vessels supposedly took to the sea in an offensive against Russia but as expected they sidetracked and went on a drinking spree.

Frestonia

Size: .0028 of a square mile

The micronation of Frestonia was established in the late 1970s when an old section of Notting Hill region of London became famous world by declaring its independence from the rest of Britain. The community, which was based on Freston Road decided to call itself Frestonia. Their main problem was that the local city council had earmarked their old houses for demolition and they were not ready to abandon their old lifestyle.

The residents simply banded together and conducted a referendum where they overwhelmingly voted for secession. They went on to declare themselves an independent state on Halloween night of 1977. Soon thereafter they applied for induction and recognition into the United Nations, warning they would actually need the services of peace keeping troops should the council try and evict them forcefully.

The media coverage that surrounded the event made it difficult for the council to fulfill their threat of evicting the Frestonians from their neighborhood. Thereafter was a public inquiry into the matter and the micronation was given a right to exist as they desired.

The residents took the bull by the horns and decided to build their own nation soon creating a national anthem, postage stamps, and even newspapers. They even had their own film institute which regularly showed concert footage of Sex Pistols. The area was soon to become a counterculture haven and come 1982, The Clash—a music group—came to the community to record their album Combat Rock.

Finally some members of the community had private negotiations with the city council in order to receive assistance to help rebuild the district that was crumbling. Frestonia therefore lost its cherished freedom and many of the original citizens moved away. It was no time before the micronation came tumbling down but even today, the neighborhood has remained a closely knit community.

Talossa

Many amateur nation builders have discovered that the internet is the veritable playground from where to start their projects. Many micronations that exist only on paper or in founders minds always use websites to publicize their intentions and more often than not to build up their populations through blogs as a way of drumming up their own support.

Flag of the Kingdom of Talossa

The best example of this is the Kingdom of Talossa, a micronation that was established in 1979 by a 14 year old teenager Robert Ben Madison from Milwaukee, Wisconsin. He claimed to have seceded from the United States that very same year but it appears that the US authorities have never been aware of the said secession.

Even though Talossa began as joke in Ben's bedroom, it established itself as a constitutional monarchy and in 1995 it became the first micronation to have its own website. It is through this website that the membership of the kingdom is said to have grown rather rapidly. The kingdom thereafter developed a cult like following and they have conventions called Talossafests which are usually held in or out of Milwaukee.

The National Snack and national drink of the Kingdom of Talossa

As far as micronations are concerned, Talossa has developed one of the most fully developed cultures. They have developed their own language and a dictionary that boast s 25,000 words in what they call the Talossan tongue. In 2004 however there was a revolt and the rebelling members formed what is today known as the Republic of Talossa.

Llanrwst

This Welsh town was declared independent of the surrounding diocese in 1276 by the last Prince of Wales Lylwelyn Gruffydd. The local pope decided to appeal to the Pope but the pope would hear none of it. There were actually four different popes that very same year of 1276 but not one of them would listen to what was happening somewhere in an English village.

The town went to create its own coat of arms, national flag as well as a motto attesting to its freedom and independence, "Wales, England and Llanrwst." They went on to appeal for recognition by the United Nations in 1947 but it remains that they were never recognized as independent state.

Seborga

Size: 4 square miles

The micronation of Seborga has a long history that sates back to the 10th century when this tiny enclave in northern Italy was given independence and then handed over to some monks so that they would build a monastery. It maintained the status quo until seven hundred years later when it was annexed by the Kingdom of Sardinia, which occupied parts of what is now Italy and Spain.

Even at the end of the Sardinian Kingdom the Italian State never go to reclaim Seborga and things went on to stay that way until 200 years later in the early 1960s when an artist, Giorgio Carbone argued that it was an independent state since it had never surrendered its autonomy. After managing to convince the town's people he was elected the head of the country of Seborga.

Things went on in the same manner until during the mid 1990s when the people of Seborga, numbering about 300 in total voted in a referendum to finally declare their town an independent state. Carbone was the official leader of the micronation until his death in 2009. He was the most prolific promoter of the republic and is responsible for instituting the country's flag, postage stamps and the motto—"sit in the shade".

Seborga Flag

The government of Italy has never recognized it as a sovereign state and so the residents of Seborga still remit their taxes to the Italian government and also attend their schools. The government though has never quite discouraged the activities that symbolically make it look like a real state and it is even known that Seborga has a standing army that consists of only a single soldier—Lt. Antonello Lacalo.

Marlborough

Marlborough is a defunct micronation that was founded in 1993 in Rockhampton, Australia and had a population of only two people. The creator of the micronation declared his farm an independent country so as to avoid eviction and bankruptcy. He was however evicted about a week later by the police and was prosecuted and that became the end his independence as a state.

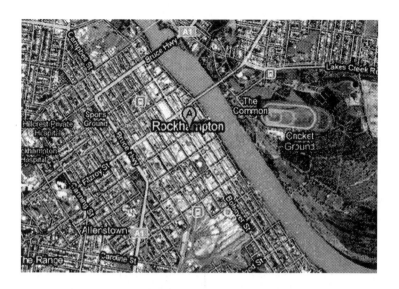

Sark

The micronation of Sark has been until very recently feudal state in Europe. It has been a crown dependency like the neighboring Guernsey and is independent of UK being run by a Lord who gave out land in return to military service. The island has been so isolated to an extent that they even developed their own language and they do not have cars instead using horse drawn carriages.

The place is also among those places that have maintained a complete smoking ban and being an idyllic place many people would covet it. It happened that in 1990 an armed nuclear physicist tried to invade and take it over but was stopped by a solitary soldier and was arrested before he could realize his dream.

Flag of Kingdom of Ark

Currently they have decided and are in the process of modernizing their enclave to make it a democracy in order to make it compatible with the European Convention of Human Rights. When some brothers who ran businesses in the island wanted to vie for the leadership, they were badly defeated in an election and ended up closing their businesses rendering about a half of the population jobless. Donations came in to help the government running and currently some businesses are opening up again.

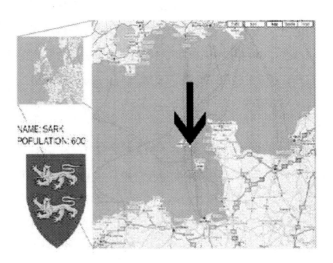

Waveland

Waveland is located in a rocky uninhabited island near the United Kingdom which is also referred to as Rockall. There has been a raging dispute regarding its ownership with countries such as United Kingdom, Iceland, Ireland as well as Denmark all claiming ownership.

The rock was briefly occupied by Greenpeace, an environmentalist organization so as to protest drilling of oil in the area and in the process declared the rock and independent state known as Waveland. It invited people to become citizens as long as they pledged their allegiance. Since the United

Kingdom considers it its territory it has allowed Greenpeace to operate from UK and they have simply ignored the declaration of independence. The protest went on until 1999 when Greenpeace lacked funding and went under and all that now remains is a solar powered beacon that helps ships avoid hitting the tiny island.

Chapter Seven

The Newest Micro Nations

Just like there is a League of Nations, the micronations are not also left far behind. The League of Micronations is an inter Micronational organizations that allow the member micronations to be able to interact with each other. The organization also helps them foster their relationships as well as promote peace and a common coexistence.

The league of micronations also exists to promote diplomatic relationships between micronations inviting all interested micronations express opinions on membership so as to provide a perfect place where member micronations can be of support to each other.

The league of micronations has zero tolerance to dictatorships and does not actually recognize them at ell, whether they are micronations or regular states belonging to the United Nations.

The other aim is to find out ways they could even interact with their bigger counterparts.

It is the aim of the league of micronations to have their members get recognition from the United Nations and become members when the time is right. When this is done they believe they will be able to open diplomatic missions all over the world and as such they are bringing together micronations that would be candidates for the recognition of favorable micronations.

Due to the many rising powers in the world, the league of micronations has identified several countries that it considers to be superpowers. To these micronations, a superpower would be defined as a country that can sustain its own stability and civility while simultaneously having an influence over several other countries in their own region and beyond and to some extent the rest of the world.

Following this definition, the league of micronations recognizes twelve countries to be superpowers and they include United States of America, Australia, the United Kingdom, Brazil, Japan, China, Indonesia, Nigeria, France, India, Russia, Egypt and Germany. These are known as super powers because they have all claimed to be super powers on some scale and all of them besides Australia, a regional powers to be reckoned with.

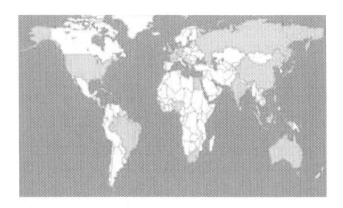

List of super powers according to league of micronations

The league of micronation does not necessarily members of the United Nations Security Council to be superpowers. They believe that it is not fair for the UN Security Council to give some powerful nations such a status making some of them more powerful than they really need to be. They believe that some of those countries they have included in their list of super powers have a say in their regions over world trade as well as other regional powers.

The league of micronations recognizes some African countries such as Nigeria, Egypt and South Africa as superpowers because according to them they are regional powers in the African Continent. A strong nation such as Ethiopia was disregarded from the list because they lack a navy for being landlocked. One requirement for a nation to be recognized as a super power by the league of micronations is to have a navy that can challenge others as well as have control over any major trade routes in the oceans. Following is a list of new and emerging micronations that will also join the league of micronations.

People's Republic of Stodaenna

The People's Republic of Stodaenna is a socialist republic with strong ties with the Swedish Monarchy and is located in Bohulsan, a small region just south of Norway. The majority of its territory is however is located in Sweden.

Because of the size of the country, it imports almost all its supplies from Sweden since there is basically no border control. Stodaenna is a primarily agricultural country with the only other industry having to do with logging. The micronation claims to be socialist, the number of imports that come from both Sweden and Norway seem to have forced the micronation to developed a mixed economy as well as have strong ties with the Swedish as well as Norwegian Monarchies but mostly that one of Sweden.

Kingdom of Theodia

The Kingdom of Theodia is an American micronation with a form of government that is a constitutional monarchy which uses the Nordic language and it also uses the Nordic alphabet. The word Theodia is actually a Nordic word translated people or nation.

Theodia is currently governed as an absolute monarchy but it is in the process of drafting a constitution. In the meantime, King Swen I, have been trying to keep peace and democracy throughout the nation and so far he seems to have succeeded. This micronation is located next to the American state of Florida and it currently has some two provinces and it is a member of the Runic Union.

People's RepublicÊWest Antarctica

The People's Republic of West Antarctica is a micronation that was previously known as the Republic of Weissland. It is a federal republic consisting of three administrative units which are not known by any official name. This is unlike other countries that would have called them states, provinces or perhaps regions. These administrative units are the Marieland, Booth Island and the Capital Territory.

The Republic of West Antarctica has a Serbian origin and the official language is therefore Serbian. The micronation is located in West Antarctica but it also lays claim on some island off the coats of the Antarctic Peninsula as the administrative unit of Booth Island.

Kingdom of Wyvern

The Kingdom of Wyvern is federal constitutional monarchy that seceded from the Netherlands and is therefore a Dutchophone nation. It is made up of seven federal states that are: Wyvern, Behemoth, Dullahan, Xtabay, the Marine State as well as the New Xtabay. Each of these federal states has its own unique capital and a specific culture.

The federal state of Marine is the only one that borders a body of water, the Atlantic Ocean. Marine is the only state that borders a body of water, the Atlantic Ocean. Most of the citizens of Wyvern, as with most European countries, are European, mainly of Dutch descent. Its national colors are Purple and Black, and its flag was made with the white bar in the center to represent the country's Dutch heritage.

Student's Isocratic Oligarchy of Yabloko

The Students isocratic Oligarchy of Yabloko is an extremely influential micronation that was founded in June 2010 and is surrounded by the Australian City of Sydney. Its system of government is a Unitary isocratic oligarchy headed by a chancellor and their official currency is a called a Yablokon Kon.

The micronation was founded by Aldrich Lucas, dissolved its parliament earlier on in its existence as a country and transformed it into an isocratic oligarchy. This is a complicated form of government that is unique to only Yabloko and it is a system in which people own a state that is ruled by a few significant citizens such as the Grand Chancellor.

The country is a unitary democratic state and is divided into five administrative areas: Apfeldstadt, Zwiebelkopfia, Pjafèl, Appuru and Raftel, each governed by an administrator.

Kingdom of Albion

The Kingdom of Albion is a unitary constitutional monarchy that was founded as the Kingdom of Dadingisila. It was however unsuccessful and that prompted its citizens to establish a new country and that is how the Democratic nation of Albion was established.

The Kingdom of Albion is made up of five islands that are located off the coast of Antractica: Vollmer, Moody, Kizer, Przbyszewski and Cronenwett Island, which are each divided into shires, with the capital city, called Center Town and which is situated on the central island, Vollmer Island. The micronation has s small population who use the Albion gold as their official currency. They have political parties which resemble those of a monarchy and are called families. The Kingdom of Albion is a member of the Flandrensisian Commonwealth.

Federated States of Antarctica

The Federal States of Antarctica is a union of seven microstates that claim a territory that has dozens of small enclaves around the Antarctic continent. It is a seamount chain in the Southern Ocean that thinks the potential of a Seasteading is going to be highly ambitious. It has a constitution that is almost a complete replica of that one of the American state of Alaska and this is where the bulk of the citizens live, waiting to relocate when the time is ripe.

Principality of Arkel

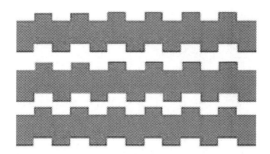

The Principality of Arkel is a micronation in the Antarctic region that is composed mainly of Dutch and Belgian citizens. The capital city of the Principality, Nieuw—Castricum is actually named after the city of Casticum, in the Netherlands.

The location of the tiny country is mostly on Dean Island but it claims some more territory on the Ross Ice Shelf which actually surrounds the island on almost all sided during the frigid Antarctic winters.

The Principality of Arkel was founded through the support of the Flandrensis and the Frandrensisian Commonwealth during October 2010. Arkel is a model unitary principality and its only external territory is the protectorate known as the Ross Ice Shelf which is made up of numerous small micro-islands. The Principality of Arkel is a member of the Flandrensisian Commonwealth.

Republic of Atlantis

The Republic of Atlantis is a micronation kingdom that was founded in 1995. It was embroiled in a number of political divisions which finally led to a civil war, which is supposed to be ongoing even to date. The country has its roots in the Italian way of life as well as the Neapolitan culture.

It is surrounded completely by the region in Italy known as Campania whose capital is Naples. The Republic of Atlantis is still embroiled in a civil war with the rebel nation of Makhnovist, which still occupies more than half of the capital city of Atlantis, Poseidon.

Republic of Emerald Isle

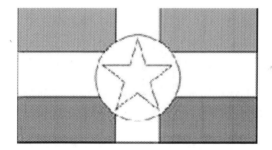

The Republic of Emerald isle is an emerging micronation that has just emerged from a transitional revolution from kingdom nation that is located on the Barrier Islands of the Outer Banks which is an island formation off the coats of North Carolina in the United States of America. The country is a strong democracy, and its government is modeled heavily after a revised version constitution and government of the United States.

Mohammad Bahareth

Transitional Government of Escitrar

A former territory of the Federal Republic of Saint Charlie, Escitrar, also known as Tammarack, followed Sandus' lead and declared its independence from the Saint Charlian commonwealth. The country's constitution is currently being rewritten, as the current constitution is too complicated to serve the country's best needs.Ê

After secession from Saint Charlie, the population doubled in a matter of weeks, with increased immigration from Saint Charlie and other Western European states. Ê4 Provinces were then formed, whose names are currently East, West, North and South Escitrar, until names are decided upon.

Grand Duchy of Flandrensis

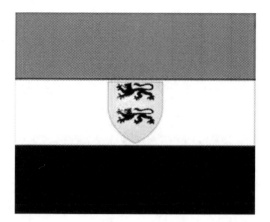

The Grand Duchy of Flandrensis is an extremely influential micronation that was founded in August 2008 and is governed as a democratic grand duchy in the Antarctica region. Flandrensis is located on some five small islands that are located off the coast of West Antarctica Siple Island, Pranke Island, Maher Island, Cherry Island and Charney Island, which are further divided into eighteen counties.

The capital of the Republic, Siple, is aptly named after the island it sits on and it is the micro nation's commercial and political hub. This is a Dutch speaking nation but most of the inhabitants or originally Belgian and Dutch nationals. The country is named after the Flanders region in Belgium. The Grand Duchy of Flandrensis is a member of the Flandrensisian Commonwealth.Ê

Kingdom of Juclandia

The Kingdom of Juclandia is one of the micronations found in Eastern Europe and also happens to be one of the most complicated forms of government. It is founded as a liberal Socialist Democracy (called the Socialist Republic of Juclandia) after the Romanian revolt against communist rule.

The micronation is made up of four administrative regions, Jucareni County, Floral County, Cipimania County and the Autonomous Region of Cainesti. Cainesti is the county that has more autonomy than the remaining three counties.

Community of Landashir

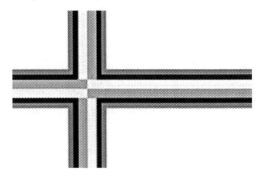

The community of Landashir was founded as the Crown
principality of Landashir before it made a swift transition to a
partisan democracy sometime in 2010. It was established in the
land the belonged to the now defunct Kingdom of Finismund.

The community of Landashir lays claim over some five islands
off the coast of Marie Byrd Land deep inside the Antarctica. It
is made up of three administrative regions namely Lanshire,
Llabdey and the Oak Department and has built a language,
based on German and Dutch called Francillish.

Federal Republic of Los Bay Petros

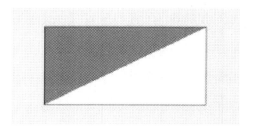

The Federal Republic of Los Bay Petros is amicronation that
was founded in 2009 as the Petrovakian Federation and with
time the country has been transformed to Los Bay Petros after
the signing of the New Petrovakian Treaty. It is among the
few micronations found in Asia, being found in the country of
Indonesia and is surrounded from every side by the capital city,
Jakarta.

Los bay Petros is a Micronational federation made up of six states, two regions and one protectorate. Los Bay Petros has one of the highest population densities of any micronation known anywhere, despite the fact that it is a new micronation.

People's Republic of Richland

The People's Republic of Richland is a democratic socialist presidential representative democratic socialist nation that is built as a representative democracy such as the one in Vietnam. This micronation has recently been subject to a lot of criticism when it attempted to annex and absorb the country of Ultamiya but then failed in the venture. Richland is known to have one of the strongest militaries of any micronation and is respected by the league of micronations as a superpower.

Caribbean Republic of Samana Cay

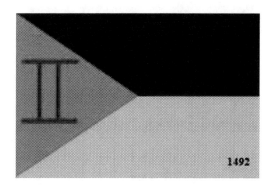

The Caribbean Republic of Samana Cay is a micronation located on Saman Cay Island which the local government also calls Aklins Island, which however is not a very common name. The reason for using the less common name is in order to avoid any confusion.

Samana Cay is considered the first site that Christopher Columbus was when he discovered America and decided to call it Guanahani. The micronation was established a commandate of Samana cay, but later there was need to form a democratic government and thatis how the Caribbean Republic of Saman Cay was founded in March 22, 2010.

State ofÊSandus

The State of Sandus is a micronation in the South Atlantic with a very strong socialist democratic ideology which was until recently a part of Saint Charlie, which was also known as the territory of Sandus or Kremlum Sandus.

The Saint Charlie did not allow Sandus to go on with its long standing socialist tradition and so the people of Sandus decided it was time to secede from the micronation of Saint Charlie and forming their own. This is what has become the People's Republic of Sandus which is a new country.

Federal Commonwealth of Sirocco

The Federal Commonwealth of Sirocco is a new micronation that is claiming territory that is also claimed by both Australia and New Zealand. It was first ruled by a dictator and was known as the Glorious Dictatorial Republic of Andersonia but was later transformed into a democracy and named Sirocco after a desert that is found in North Africa since its Australian Territory is covered by desert as well.

The micronation is a federal republic that is divided into six provinces which are also feather subdivided into different zones and principalities. In those languages where the word commonwealth is not used, Sirocco is known as the Federal Republic of Sirocco even though it is not really a commonwealth.

Republic of Subenia

The Republic of Subenia or Subenija is a micronation located in some of the islands of the Antarctica and whose capital and main locations are on the island of Dustin.

It borrows its name from the Greek word for the Slavic people of the Balkans, Subenoi, which is well and good since the country is actually based in Serbia. Subenia insists that it is not a micronation and that it has all the qualifications of a nation as outlined in the Montevideo Convention and wants to be recognized as a sovereign nation.

The Republic of Subenia has a flag that is similar to those of majority of the Balkan nations with the prominent colors being white, red and blue with an imperial eagle which was left over from the ancient days of the Austrian Empire.

Talossan Republic

The Republic of Talossa is a micronation that is a breakaway from the Kingdom of Talossa, another micronation. The Republic of Talossa broke away to the north in 2004 and became a free democratic country after the monarch of the Kingdom of Talossa was repeatedly accused of abusing his power. The Talossan Republic is notable among micronations because it speaks anew language that was constructed from scratch and is spoken by many citizens of the country as the official language.

People's Republic of Tiana

The People's Republic of Tiana is a micronation that is a democratic socialist constitutional presidential republic that was formerly known as the Federation of Tiana's Socialist Republics. It is located in the United States and borders the American State of New York in the American East Coast.

The Peoples Republic of Tiana is made up of three provinces which all have the name Socialist Republic in front of their names: Tiana, Flanders and Atlantica. There are plans to introduce another new province to be called the Socialist Republic of Great Neck.

Mohammad Bahareth

Kingdom of West Germania

The Kingdom of West Germania is micronation in the British Isles that is located very close to the City of York in England. This is a kingdom that is centered on the Celtic and Germanic cultures of the British Isles, Scandinavia and North Europe.

The micronation has two dominant religions which are Christianity and Germanic paganism which are very rare and often misunderstood religions elsewhere. The official language is West Germanic which is a direct descendant of the Old English Language and just like the relationship between Portuguese and Spanish, old English speakers could understand and write what a West Germanic is saying and vice versa. The Kingdom of West Germania is a member of the Runic Union.

Holy Salanian Empire

The Republic of Salania was founded on July 8, 2008 as a
Parliamentary Republic. It became the Holy Salanian Empire
on July 10, 2010 in a special session of Parliament. Though
now an Imperialist Monarchy, Salania still has a Parliament and
a Bill of Rights to protect its citizens from oppression. The Holy
Salanian Empire is a Commonwealth Realm.

After it's formation, the Republic was almost immediately
embroiled in a week-long Civil War, and then a two month
war with a neighboring micronation. After weathering these
terrible affairs, Salania entered a period of stagnation, ended
by the third and most devastating war, which almost resulted in
complete capitulation.

The Republic eventually became the Holy Salanian Empire,
as of July 10, 2010, though it still retains several elements of a
democracy.

The Empire participated in the Second War for Victoria for
approximately half an hour. The Empire ceded a vast amount
of new land, including the Kingdom of Milligansa, on August
27, 2010. The Empire participated in the War of the Forest in

support of its ally, the UPUC. The Empire remained loyal to the President in the Atlantis Civil War and currently supports the Loyalist cause. The Empire is currently supporting Zurdonia in the War for Oceanland.

The Tsarist Empire of Gishabrun

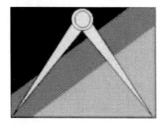

Gishabrun officially The Tsarist Empire of Gishabrun, is a small constitutional monarchy bordering Canada, the U.S.A. and Russia and was founded for three main reasons;

"The first is to preserve the natural environment and to execute such actions in a more effective manner than the Dominion of Canada and the Russian Federation currently are. The second is to give every ethnic and religious group in our glorious nation a large portion in government and to keep all traditions of these groups alive and for these groups to stay separate and distinct. The third and last reason is to build a better and more lawful government than the one currently existing in Canada and Russia."

The Empire is led by a Tsar, currently HIM Kuri I, and prides itseslf in being one of the few micronations ruled by one. The

Empire is very science-focused and the advancement of the sciences, especially biology and ecology, is almost always the top priority for the Empire. The Empire is also quite socialist as it denounces all forms of capitalism and supports socialist ideas and philosophies.

Union of South London Soviet Socialist Republics

The Union of South London Soviet Socialist Republics, also known as the USLSSR, is a socialist union located in South London. It is made up of a collection of bedrooms in and around places such as the Lewisham and Greenwich boroughs. An easy way to gain citizenship without knowing a current citizen is to serve in the Foreign Legion of the USLSSR.

Federal Republic of St. Charlie

The federal Republic of St. Charlie is a territorial European micronation located in Italy and is a member of the Grand Unified Micronational as well as the organization of Active Micronations. Even though it is located in Italy, it spreads to a good part of Southern Europe with some of its territories located in countries such as Germany and the British Isles. St. Charlie is a parliamentary presidential federal republic that was founded in 2008 with a single party system that was later abolished in 2009.

By far, this is the largest micronation in Italy by area and of course one of the few that are found in Italy. This micronation has been a major power with a strong foundation in areas like the economy, political and cultural influence. St. Charlie became a symbol unity and micronationalism in a high school in London.

The micronation was ruled by a monarchy from its inception in late 2000 until November 2008 when the ruling monarch decided to abdicate due to health challenges. The monarchy was officially dissolved on the 15th of that month and libertarian revolution began which was supported by a number of citizens.

There was however a counter revolution by those who strongly supported a monarchy who managed to crush it initially. However, on the 20th of that month Alexander Reinhardt and Whisky I took control of the royal palace and established the National Party before they dissolved the Kingdom.

They took the following three days to draft the constitution and the new St. Charlie was born as well as establishing a new currency known as the Pineta. The new constitution was promulgated on the 23rd and that led to the establishment of the federal republic.

Slinky Empire

The Slinky Empire which is also known as the Slinky Parliamentarian Monarchy is a micronation that is based in Europe and North America. It shares borders with the Unite States of America, the United Kingdom of Great Britain, the Dominion of Canada, the Empire of Austenasia, Republic of Ireland, republic of North Ireland, the Republic of Malta and the Federal Republic of Rukora. The current ruler is the founder of the empire, Kyng Fyrst.

The Slinky Empire was established on December 31st 2008 when Kyng Fyrst signed the Slinky Document thereby establishing the Slinky Parliamentary Monarchy. That is the document that lays the foundation of the republic and it includes the name, type of government, emblem, rues of parliament as well as the royalty.

There is also another document known as The ten Crymes Document which lays out ten heinous crimes that will not go unpunished if they are done intentionally. The ten crymes are: torture, murder, adultery, fraud, discrimination, vagrancy, theft, disobedience, overwork, and gluttony.

The Ten Laws document which was signed into law in 2009 also goes further to explain the Slinky law and also limits the powers of the parliament as well as the Kyng. It also lays out the roles of all the citizens and explains the process of going to war among other things. All citizens of the Slinky Empire have ten rights that cannot be taken away and these are: the right to believe anything, the right to have fun, the right to be happy, and the right to learn.

It is the business of Kyng Fyrst to sign certificates of approval to do business in the Kingdom. Among the documents he signed in 2009 included The Slinky Treasury, and this was followed by Education and tourism. Then in June 2009 there was the approval of the Slinky Police Business which was later followed by the Slinky Air Force.

All long tern decisions in the Slinky Empire are written and signed in a from known as The form of Royal Proclamations and according to the law there cannot be more than 100 royal proclamations in effect at any one time. There are a total of 400 royal proclamations that are in effect currently.

The Heptarchy of New Herakleia

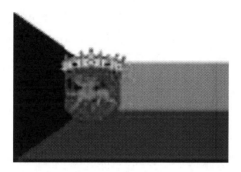

The Heptarchy of new Herakleia is a Greek micronation that seceded from Greece in 2010 even though it was established way back in 2006by seven Greek citizens who wanted to live by their own right and ways. Over the following two years after the establishment there was a great evolution in the level of self government that they enjoyed which led to a practical provision of a government with its own local customs in the village of Nea Heraklia in Chalkidiki.

The idea of a secession emerged in 2009 and this lead to amore organized central government which was followed by a declaration of independence a year later during which the constitution was signed.

The government of the Heptrarchy of New Herakleia has evolved through the years to form a multi-factional system of laws which are extremely simple in principle following a decentralized approach to all the rulings of the upper house and supporting the lower house.

While the upper house is responsible for the creation and enforcement of laws, the lower house mainly functions as a court of law. The lower house also has power to veto or edit the decisions of the upper house most of the time except in a few constitutional cases. The borders are open to anyone who wishes to take up citizenship and who will be issued with a business passport. It is the business of the Bureau of Foreigners to facilitate citizenship although there are no standard qualifications that are required for one to qualify.

Empire of New Europe

The Empire of new Europe is a North American based Micronation which is a federal constitutional monarchy of over twenty states. The founder member of the Triune Alliance has its headquarters in Chicago. It is one of the micronations that have dedicated it self to improving the lot of micronations that are found in the United States of America.

The Empire of new Europe was founded by three people whose aim was to secure a bright future for Americans of European descent as well as those living in Canada. It originally began as a white supremacist movement that was bent on sticking to ethnic cleansing and racial superiority. However, as the membership grew and more activism started by other members apart from those original three, they were forced to distance themselves from racism as much as possible.

The European Republic of New Europe had begun as a fascist dictatorship which originally only admitted European Americans of German descent. The increase of membership and activities forced later on to open their doors to all other Europeans. The Germans also held leadership positions until late 2009 when the members called for more action and integration, demanding a national vote to determine the future of the republic.

At this time the kingdom had more monarchists than fascists and the leader of the group ended up being crowned the Emperor. The newly crowned Emperor Wilhelm Kaiser then decided to establish the Empire of New Europe and later made their first contact with Micronational community in January 2009.

People Reformed States Republic

The People's reformed States Republic was originally established as a monarchy on 1st may 2009 with the name the Royal Reformed States of America. It was later reformed to a monarchy the 1st June 2010 as it is today. The micronation runs a system known as A1ism and it remains only other one of only two nations who do, the other one with the same system of government is a micronation called the Most Glorious Republic of A1. The state is headed by a Chancellor and the current one is His Excellence James Willary.

The one thing that is different about the People's Reformed States Republic is that unlike most other republics, the country does not have any special or unique name. This is the same case with the A1 as is found in the Most Glorious People's Republic of A1 as well as Zonian for the Zonian confederacy.

The system recommends that the name be made up of completely descriptive terms. The main reason for this is that when the original Royal Reformed States of America was founded, they could not find a reasonable name and so decided to leave it without a specific name.

United People under Chance

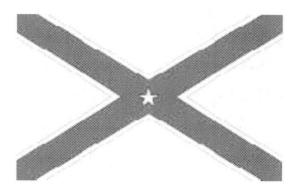

The United Provinces under Chance, is an American micronation claiming thirteen independently owned properties in California, two properties in Alabama, one in Minnesota and Maine, an intergalactic colony, an Irish Colony and five territories. The original micronation fell in September 2010 and was reestablished as a more democratic state called the Kingdom of Zurdonial. The United People Under Chance has a population of 52 people and it is trying to create diplomatic relations with any other micronations it believes are as strong as it is.

The country is currently run by a military Junta which also controls any business ventures by the citizens. There official religion of the UPUC is Christianity even though no one is forced to join it or any other religion for that matter.

Mohammad Bahareth

The Republic of Wickliffia

The Republic of Wickliffia is a micronation based in North America that consists of 6 states and two territories. The Capital is Orlanda which is located in the State of Ridgewick. Wicklifia claims to be a great ally of USA and it actually aids them in war they could get involved in. the nations however claims to behaving a problem with a high crime rate especially in Northern Ridgewick.

The origin of Wickliffia is traced back to the time when Americans moved west from the colonies and established the State of Ohio. When the Italians wanted to control a piece of territory north east of Cleveland in the 1820s, they were given a piece of land and they built a military base in what is now called labyrinth Territory. Finally Italian citizens moved and established towns and villages.

It is the Italians who established the Wickliffia Territory and thereafter the economy began to prosper. However, some twenty years later the economy began to deteriorate and the residents of Wickliffia wanted to have their freedom and this is what originated the Italian—Wickliffian war.

The United States came to the aid of Wickliffia and fought with them in the war for the territory. Two years later Wickliffia declared independence and two more states were formed; Lincoln and Ridgewick. The other four states have been formed over the years so that there are now six states and two territories.

Chapter Eight

You can start Your Own Micronation

This may come as a surprise to you but the truth of the matter is that you can actually start your own country. If you are simply sick of paying taxes to a government that does not deliver services and the leaders are corrupt liars, or may be you just don't like the system of government you find yourself in, the answer could be as simple as starting your own country and declaring yourself king or president for life.

It is actually simpler that you may want to believe, thanks to modern land moving technology. However, the undertaking itself may not be as simple as it sounds but it can still be done. History has it that from time immemorial people have built artificial islands for many reasons: to create homes, self defense against wild animals and other tribes. Even today there people who have created new islands for settlement and other infrastructure.

A perfect example is the country of Japan the flattened a nearby mountain and dumped it in an island site so as to build what is today the Kansai International Airport at Osaka Bay. The same things have happened in places such as Hong Kong, who enlarged an existing island so as to accommodate a new airport and expand existing bridges spending an entire 15 Billion Dollars in the process.

In some primitive cases, villagers have built structures on stilts over shallow water and created homes that would not have actually been there. Some of the most prominent cases are to be found in the Upper Amazon basin in countries such as Peru, Brazil and in Borneo. There is an interesting village of textile workers built in the middle of a lake in northern Myanmar.

One of the most prominent artificial islands of modern times is found in the United Arab Emirates in what is called the Burj Al-Arab Hotel that has been built on an artificial island in Dubai. It was later followed by the building of the famous Palm Island group that employed the best creative design and has actually become a centerpiece of excellence in architectural design and construction.

This has given an impetus to people with ideas of creating micronations who have come up with numerous ventures in trying to establish their own dreams into reality. Modern utopias in people's minds will sooner rather than later become reality if the quest for personal freedom that people seek is anything to go by. Many people look forward to developing their own tax havens and cities of pleasure and all those are now glaring possibilities.

Since most of the land all over the world seems to have already been claimed by one nation or another, founders of micronations are considering the international waters as the next stop for them. A good example is the principality of Sealand which is built on an abandoned Second World War gun platform off the coast of England. Many developers are looking for sites that can be claimed and they are not sparing coral reefs and other under ocean-mountains that can be raised quickly.

The future of new country projects therefore seems to lie in building artificial islands in the international waters as this has proven to be a practical venture already. With the development in building technology there is only your imagination and the requisite funds that could stop you from realizing your dream of beginning your own country where you become the supreme leader and lay down the rules.

Start Your Own Country

After reading this book so far you may have developed an idea to create your own country. You may have seen tens of reasons why people got dissatisfied with the existing systems and decided to begin the process of creation of their own countries. Even though some may have sounded like jokers, it still goes on to talk about the dissatisfaction people have with current systems of governance in the world. If you really desire to build your own tiny country, tighten your seat belt and let us walk you through the process.

Before you set yourself up to the creation of your own micronation it may be important to first of all remind yourself of what a micronation really is.

Definition:

"A micronation is an entity created and maintained as if it were a nation and/or a state, and generally carrying with it some, most or all of the attributes of nationhood, and likewise generally carrying with it some of the attributes of statehood. Though a micronation may well have begun as a mere drollery, it has the potential (given the evolution of a sufficiently vital national culture) to develop into a true nation, and possibly to achieve statehood."

Peter Ravn Rasmussen

Or may be the definition of a micronation from the Kingdom of Talossa may suffice:

"Micronations, microstates, imaginary countries, countercountries, unrecognized nations, or ephemeral states, are all terms for countries which have been declared independent by (usually eccentric) individuals or small groups, but unlike other such attempts, fail to achieve widespread diplomatic recognition. Many have only one inhabitant; others are larger. Most seem to consist of a single Grand Poobah, with or without a coterie of petits Poobahs. Talossa, however, counts over 50 citizens who have been part of its wild multiparty political structure. And there are reportedly 20,000 people with Hutt River citizenship or honors—more than several members of the UN!"

In many cases that we have gone through in this book so far, people who established micronations claimed territories that already existed under the dominion of other existing republics; more often than not some small uninhabited islands which could even have been under water at times.

Some micronations have gone further to declare independence, developed and adopted constitutions, sought international recognition and in some cases even sent out envoys. Others have issued passports, produced postage stamps as well as having flags and coats of arms as well as minting their own currencies. After getting a definition of what a micronation is then there is no reason why we should not get into the process.

First Things First

If you have harbored feelings of dissatisfaction with your country and wondering whether it is time you started your own, then you are not alone. There are many people who had the same feelings but not so many of them went on to actualize their dreams. You can actually join the league of those few imaginative minds that forge ahead and create a path where there was none and end up with a real country they have created from scratch.

Having made up your mind that this is the way you really want to go, you must ask yourself exactly what your goal is or else you will just end up where you started if not worse. There are different types of micronations like we have already seen earlier in this book which are all started for different reasons. In a book entitled "How to Start Your Own Micronation" by Erwin S. Strauss we are given five different categories which will serve our purpose as well.

- "Traditional sovereignty: Having status as a sovereign nation, including exchanging ambassadors, acceptance of passports, membership in international organizations. This usually includes possession of actual territory (land).

- Ship under flag of convenience: Ships off the coast of sovereign nations, usually as part of a money-making scheme.

- Litigation: Using macronational law to press your claim to independence.

- Vonu (out of sight out of mind): Establishing your "nation" in a remote area, far from macronational authority.

- Model country: A project nation designed to resemble most aspects of nationhood, without actually seeking sovereignty. Generally this is the definition of an on-line nation."

In order to understand this further we will also quote Lars Erik Bryld, he of the Sovereign principality of Corvinia who does a further breakdown that will be important especially for those who are extremely serious in building a micronation that could become a state sometime in the near future.

- Statehood: acquisition and complete control over a territory, and the acceptance of this sovereignty by the international society.

- Nationhood: a condition where a group of persons achieve a common identity as a people and the will to be identified as such.

- A Political Exercise: the attempt to create a plausible and internally consistent simulation of a governmental mechanism. Though the ultimate purpose might be recreational, emphasis is on the realism.

- Community: a society of like-minded individuals, which in some respects does not possess the attributes of a nation as defined above.

- Fun: a completely spurious vehicle of interacting as a way of entertainment. Though a governmental structure may exist, the prime purpose is to have fun.

The first important step therefore is to ask yourself exactly why you want to start a new micronation. Even though most people begin micronation projects just for fun, there are those that evolve and end becoming serious at the end of the day. It is therefore paramount that you have a really good reason or at least know why you want to get into this kind of project as a starting point.

No matter what goals you have in mind as you begin your new country project, knowing where you are going will help you deal with any challenges that could arise anywhere along the way. Therefore think and plan ahead for your micronation project to see the light of the day.

There are hundreds of Micronational projects going on right now for all manner of reasons. Whether the reasons are good or questionable, it is the seriousness that you give your effort that will determine whether your project will see the light of the day or not. Many micronation projects that succeed are usually anchored in reasons that are as close to reality as possible.

You must therefore do all in your ability to avoid dealing in issues that are based in spurious reasons as well as fictional materials. If you are looking for actual independence and in the process you manage to convince a few other people to go along with you then you will be in a better position to succeed than those who base their inspiration on fiction and have imaginary citizens who support them in their cause. You do not want to get into any venture that will spoil your chances of becoming a sovereign nation in future if that is really your goal.

The seriousness you employ in your venture will go along way in determining whether you succeed or not. The reception you receive from other microantionalists could be varied but with a burning goal in your mind you will not let those negative people deter you from your progress. Friends and family are also likely to either support you or ridicule you and laugh themselves lame over your idea. Stick to your goal if you really are serious about what you have set yourself to do.

The Fundamental Issues

If you have read up to this point you may want to have ideas on how to really start your own country. The simple basics that you need are in order. The first things you will need are citizens and because we live in the era of the internet you need your own website. The website is extremely important because many micronations have a website and that is everything there is.

It may be possible for you to start without any citizens and the website will come in handy because you can use it to sell your goals and policies. However, there are people who want to establish countries without having to share them with anyone else. The good thing about it all is that when you build up a country and website that are attractive, you are most likely to attract people to become citizens.

You need to have something interesting and exciting. You need to influence people with goals that are going to be beneficial to them. You need to make a difference in people's hopes; aspirations and expectations or else you will join the league of one man micronations that are all over the net.

Take extreme care also that you do not have your website as the nation because that is likely to happen. The website should only be a tool, a means to an end and not the end itself. It should be your means of communicating with the rest of the world and as a matter of principle your nation must exist beyond your online presence. Failure to do this will lead you to having such a hard time selling your idea while at the same time people will not take you too seriously.

You may want to start out by surveying how other micronations have presented themselves on the internet before you build your own website. If you don't want to spend any money at the beginning you may want to consider some free web hosting services. Look at their symbols, flags, coats of arms as well as the descriptions of their creeds, cultures, government styles and citizenship.

It will be a good thing for you to get ideas from them so that you get an idea as well how you will build yours. You may do well and good to get their ideas but avoid copying and pasting them because this could lead you to violation of people's copyrighted materials. You may need to find out what materials you may want to borrow and use with permission from the owners of the websites as long as you remember to give credit where it is due.

After you have developed your website and put your ideas on it, you need to think about important national symbols. You need to have your country's own flag since this is a major symbol of any nation. Think about the flag carefully because your flag actually represents your nation and you may need to fly it. Look at the flags that already exist and ask about what the color scheme symbolizes so that you get ideas on how to set yours up.

The reason you must take time to think about your flag is because if you are serious about building a nation that will pass the test of time, you must be seen to be having a level permanence. Changing the flag too often will make people wonder whether you were serious from the word go. When you avoid making numerous changes now and again it may help you to help play off diplomatically and your nation will give an appearance of stability.

You will thereafter need to think about the coat of arms for your republic. It is not such a big deal making up your coat of arms if you have any little knowledge of graphic design. Your coat of arms, just like your flag, should be representative of your nation. Just like the flag, look at other nations' coats of arms so as to get ideas about what direction to take in this matter.

The other important symbols you may have to consider will include a national anthem, national food, national animal or even a national bird if you think it necessary. Whatever you think is best must of necessity represent your nation and its goals and themes. Think about the possibility of adopting a country theme that you will identify with and that your citizenry will love to be identified with as well.

A good sign of a country that is serious is the ownership of land that you will have either bought or even lay claim on. The land you claim may not necessarily be yours and can actually be some public land. Some people have tried to claim public utility land such as public parks, national parks or even a nature reserve. They take pictures of these places and post them on the internet and that helps them to create interest from people interested in citizenry.

As a nation, you need to make others think that your nation actually exists. Post announcements about activities that your nation has been having such as elections, coronations and etc. try and create ministries and departments as you appoint people to head all these different entities. Most people expect a nation to be more than just a government but also have activities that involve the government and its citizens.

The other thing a good nation will do is to have diplomatic relations with other nations and when possible get involved in foreign trade. You need to make up things your country has produced and have them sold to another nation as you also buy from other nations who will become your nation's trading partners. Also talk about sports, entertainment as well as international tournaments you plan to participate in as a nation.

Some people have created micronations and even entered into community service ventures and posted pictures on their official websites just to get publicity. The other alternative is of course to do a small activity and invite the local press to have a few paragraphs in local newspapers. What you will have done is to create curiosity and this will give you the publicity you are looking for.

If your local town has a parade of any kind for one reason or another, you may want to enlist your nation to participate. All you want to do is to create the publicity you require which will lead to inquiries that will give you potential of getting people interested in your idea as well as citizenry. Once you have something that will take you away from your office or your computer to do something about your country, you will be started on your way to realizing your dreams of establishing a new country.

The Government

Your next point should of course to have a running government that will run your micronation and hopefully, help in establishing the country you intend to establish finally. If you have political simulations with purposes of practicing the workings of a government, you then need to begin with a small entity to manage your micronation.

Depending on the government structure you fathom you may also want to establish a monarchy where all things in the government are upon you as the king of your empire. It is in cases of monarchies where the government plays a minor role in the day to day business of managing the affairs of the state. Remember, with every system of government that you decide to have you will have people interested in it and that way you are likely to attract a citizenry.

Remember that people will be watching to see if they are interested in the things you are propagating as a government before they decide whether they should join you or not. If you present a fascist, dictatorial or even communist style of government, people may fear getting associated with you because of the amount of psychological baggage associated with systems. This will also affect the kind of people you will interest as well as your standing in the league of micronations.

The league of micronations have displayed a zero tolerance towards any government systems that tend towards dictatorship and are a bit slow on communist tendencies, even though they can be accepted somehow. However, fascists will have a harder time selling their policies and as such you will be careful what impression you give to your potential citizens. The league of micronation seems to be populated with republics and monarchies which seem to be people's favorites.

It is important to design your country in such a way that you become easily accepted in the community of nations because this is always a goal that all nations seek after. The design of your micronation and its government should be in such a way that you will attract people and at the same time you will be happy and comfortable to be associated with its ideals. Even though you do your best to have something attractive, do not imagine for one moment that you are going to please everybody.

Diplomatic Relations

Diplomacy has been defined by Webster as:

"The art and practice of conducting international relations, as happens in negotiating alliances, treaties and agreements.

"The tact and skill in dealing with people"

When dealing with micronations it is important to know that diplomacy is a significant issue. When a new nation is emerging diplomatic relations is something that it must do everything to acquire. You therefore need to take a close look at the nations that you intend to start relations with. In that case you will not just accept to have diplomatic relations with just about any nation without giving them any due consideration.

As a rule of the thumb you will want to seek diplomatic relations with those nations who share almost similar ideals and concepts like yours. It is also a good idea to have relations with those micronations whose concepts and ideas will not hurt yours because generally there is something you are likely to learn from the experience.

It is important to become as formal as possible when seeking for diplomatic relations. Many people who establish micronations make a mistake to assume that the other party will appreciate relating informally. When it comes to something as important as diplomatic relations, it is safer to err on the side of truth and therefore assume the opposite and be formal.

Good diplomatic practice involves the use of a standard mail format, heading, salutation, body, closing and signature. If an informal relationship develops later between you and another micronation then informality is allowed. But the rule of the thumb remains: always be formal when dealing with another micronation.

You must therefore remember at all times that you represent a nation and not just any other entity. You will have had your own country and if you are going to make it or lose it, it will depend on how you play your game. Behave with seriousness all the time and act as if your nation was real and you will gain the respect of your peers and have a respectful standing in the world of micronations.

Mohammad Bahareth

A Model Diplomatic Letter

Foreign Ministry,

Kingdom of . . .

To:

Hon. . . .

Foreign Minister,

Republic of . . .

Your Excellency, Greetings:

This message is in reply to your message regarding diplomatic relations between out two great nations. I am quite pleased to announce that, with the approval of His Majesty, King . . . XXVIII, the Kingdom of . . . would be quite amenable to the formalization of diplomatic relations with the Republic of . . .

An exchange of ambassadors will be the natural next step in the diplomatic process. Please contact me at your earliest convenience to make arrangements for this exchange.

Respectfully,

Foreign Minister,

Kingdom of . . .

Model Constitution

This is a rather preliminary effort in putting together a very basic sample constitution which covers all essential elements while still containing as little text as possible. }

Preamble Foundation of the State

The People, pursuing the goals spelled out in this Constitution, establish the State in the Territory.

Chapter I State Definition

Article 1 State People (Citzenship, Language)

(1) Citizens of the State are all humans who are children of a citizen of the State, who are born in the Territory of the State, or who are naturalized.

(2) The official language in the State is the Language.

Article 2 State Form

(1) This State is a secular, sovereign, and democratic republic. All entities of the State must yield to these principles.

(2) This Constitution is the supreme law of the land; it is directly binding on all State authority. The general rules of public international law constitute an integral, inviolable part of the national law.

Article 3 State Symbols, Capital

(1) The State has the National Colors, the State Flag, Seal, and Coat of Arms as well as the National Anthem.

(2) The State Motto is "Liberty, Equality, Solidarity."

(3) The capital of the State is the Capital.

Chapter II State Objectives

Article 4 General Constitutional Objectives

(1) The State promotes justice and universal protection of human rights as individual rights. The State encourages fraternity among its citizens by establishing solidarity, general welfare, and national unity.

(2) The State acknowledges the right of the People to national autonomy and self-determination, and the right of minorities to group autonomy.

(3) The State promotes:

(a) public health care;

(b) education and schooling;

(c) schemes for social welfare;

(d) preservation and development of culture;

(e) preservation and maintenance of historical objects;

(f) environmental protection, intergenerational equity, and the protection of nature for its intrinsic value including the protection of nature's right;

(g) natural and social sciences.

Article 5 State Security

(1) The State promotes worldwide peace. Acts undertaken to prepare war or to otherwise disturb the peaceful relations between nations are unconstitutional.

(2) The State takes adequate measures to preserve its integrity even in the state of war or civil war.

(3) The State protects the People against terrorism, extremism, and catastrophes.

Chapter III State Organization

Part I General Organization

Article 6 Elections

(1) Absent of special provisions, elections are universal, direct, free, equal, and secret.

(2) Elections are always free and equal.

(3) Elections are always secret if a person eligible to vote or be elected so demands.

(4) Elected representatives are only bound by their conscience. They are servants of all, not only of their constituents.

Article 7 Organizational Principles

(1) The State separates executive, legislative, and adjudicative powers. Offices in different powers are incompatible with each other (horizontal imcompatibility). Offices in national entities are incompatible with any public office on a lower level (vertical incompatibility) and with any other salaried office, private or public

(economic incompatibility). Political offices are incompatible with active duty in the armed forces (military incompatibility).

(2) The State acknowledges national, regional, and local autonomy.

(3) Autonomy is bound to the principle of democratic organization.

Article 8 Decentralization, Mutual Assistance

(1) State powers belong to the Regions if not assigned to the national entities by this Constitution.

(2) The Regions are bound to convey powers to the Communes if adequate use of those powers is possible on the local level (self-government).

(3) All powers of the State have to render each other legal and administrative assistance.

Article 9 Regional Council

(1) The regions are represented in the Regional Council.

(2) The Regional Council consists of 100 members. Each region is represented in proportion to its share of citizens eligible to vote; at least by two members.

(3) Members of the Regional Council serve for a term of four years; they may be re-elected once.

(4) Every two years, the regions replace half of their members.

Article 10 National Powers

(1) State powers belong to the national entities for the following subject matters: a) state defence, b) foreign relations, c) economic regulations, d) infrastructure and traffic, e) taxation, f) solidarity systems, g) private, criminal, and procedural law, h) educational and other standards, i) and all other subject matters which by their very

nature or as a corollary to the subjects listed have to be centralized on the national level.

(2) The State may give up sovereign powers to international or supranational bodies, including systems of mutual collective security and trade organisations, as long as it retains an adequate representation in those bodies and those bodies guarantee sufficient legal protection for the Citizens.

Part II Representation of the State

Article 11 Head of State

(1) The President is the head of state. He or she has the right of pardon, to conduct foreign affairs, and to all other representative functions of the State.

(2) The President and Vice-President are elected by the National Parliament with precedence over all other business.

(3) Every resident citizen with the right to vote who has attained the age of thirty-five is eligible for the office of President or Vice-President.

(4) Before taking office, President and Vice-Presidents take the following Oath or Affirmation: "I do solemnly swear (or affirm) that I will faithfully execute this office, honoring and protecting the Constitution of the State."

(5) The President shall not be held accountable for actions performed in the exercise of his office except in the case of high treason, may be indicted only by the National Parliament, and shall be tried only by the Supreme Court.

Part III Executive Power

Article 12 National Government, President

(1) The executive power of the State is vested in the national Government. It includes diplomatic affairs.

(2) The President is the head of the National Government. The President freely chooses the National Ministers.

(3) The President is Commander in Chief of the Armed Forces.

Article 13 Impeachement

An impeachement of the President by the National Parliament takes the form of a new presidential election.

Article 14 Regional Equalization of Finances

The State provides for an overall equalization of finances, giving due consideration to the regions' repective debts, burdens, economic power, and infrastructural responsibilities.

Part IV Legislative Power

Article 15 National Parliament

(1) The legislative power is vested in the National Parliament.

(2) The National Parliament consists of 200 members. Members of the National Parliament are residents publicly elected by the People. Each region elects among its residents in proportion to its share of

citizens eligible to vote. Their office ends after a five-year term or when they lose their electoral rights.

(3) Everyone eligible to vote has recourse to the Supreme Court for scrutiny of the elections.

(4) The national parliament draws up its own rules of procedures and elects a parliamentary president and parliamentary vice###presidents.

(5) Decisions of the National Parliament require a majority of the votes cast (simple majority) unless this Constitution provides otherwise.

Article 16 Rights of Members of Parliament

(1) Members of Parliament are only bound by their consience.

(2) Members of Parliament may not be subjected to court proceedings or disciplinary action for a vote cast or a statement made by them in the National Parliament or in any of its committees (Indemnity).

(3) Members of Parliament may not be called to account or be arrested except by permission of the National Parliament (Immunity).

(4) Members of Parliament are entitled to adequate remuneration ensuring their independence. The remuneration may not be altered for the present term.

Article 17 Lawmaking Process

(1) Bills can be introduced only by the Members of Parliament or by one percent of the citizens (Public Initiative). Bills can specify the additional requirement of a public referendum after they have been voted upon.

(2) The Regional Council has to be informed immediately of any bill introduced. Members of the Regional Council have the right to be heard during sessions according to the same rules as govern the participation of Members of Parliament.

(3) Laws altering this Constitution require two thirds of the votes cast (qualified majority), at least the votes of a majority of the Members of Parliament (absolute majority). All laws are void if they are unconstitutional.

(4) Laws have to specify their effective date. They are countersigned without scrutiny by the Parliamentary President and promulgated in the Official National Publication.

(5) Bills can be submitted to a referendum if provided by parliamentary decision or as part of the initiative.

Article 18 Budget

(1) The bill for the yearly budget law is introduced by the President.

(2) Budget laws are not subjected to referendums.

Article 19 Treaties

(1) The President signs treaties with other states.

(2) The legislative power of the National Parliament includes the power to ratify treaties with other states.

(3) Treaties not ratified within six months have to be revoked by the President.

Article 20 National Ordinances

(1) Laws may empower National Ministers to adopt National Ordinances regarding a specified subject matter.

(2) National Ordinances do not require ratification by Parliament.

Article 21 State of Emergency

(1) In cases of grave and immediate threat to the existence of the State, the President may take necessary measures of defence.

(2) All emergency measures must be confirmed or revoked by the Parliament at the earliest time possible. The President is bound by the Parliaments' decisions.

Article 22 Ombudsman

The parliamentary Ombudsman safeguards fundamental rights and liberties and controls the compliance of all state powers with the provisions of this Constitution.

Part V Adjudicative Power

Article 23 Independent Courts

(1) The adjudicative power is vested in independent courts.

(2) Judges are citizens elected by the parliament. They are independent. Their office ends at time of retirement or when they lose their electoral rights.

Article 24 Supreme Court

(1) The Supreme Court decides issues involving this Constitution. In particular, the Supreme Court has jurisdiction over: a) disputes between state entities concerning their respective rights and duties under this Constitution; b) challenges of a national or regional entity,

a Court in the course of its determination, or a third of the Members of Parliament against the constitutionality of a law; c) claims of individuals regarding violations of their constitutional rights; d) popular complaints about the violation of fundamental rights; e) challenges of an act of a state power by the Ombudsman; f) cases on appeal from National Courts as the Supreme Court deems necessary to review; g) all other cases assigned to its jurisdiction by law.

(2) Decisions of the supreme court are directly binding for all entities of the State.

(3) The office of Supreme Court Justices does not exceed a period of 15 years.

Article 25 National Courts

(1) National courts have supreme jurisdiction over review and other matters assigned to it by law.

(2) Separate national courts shall be established for private law, penal law, and general public law.

(3) The supreme court decides by extraordinary review in cases of inconsistent application of the law by different national courts.

Chapter IV Fundamental Rights

Part I General Provisions

Article 26 Human Rights

(1) The State acknowledges liberty and equality of all humans.

(2) Human dignity must be respected in any case.

(3) Everyone is free to do or not to do whatever he or she chooses. Everyone is responsible for acts freely chosen.

(4) Slavery is abolished.

Article 27 Applicability

(1) Fundamental rights apply to natural persons, domestic and foreign, who are assigned these rights. They apply to legal persons, domestic and foreign, where, and to the extent that, the nature of the rights permits.

(2) Fundamental rights are inviolable and inalienable. They include the freedom not to make use of them (negative freedom). Their exercise may, in single instances, be waved by free and responsible declaration of the rightholder, but such declaration is never binding for future instances.

Part II Liberties and Property

Section I Integrity

Article 28 Personal Integrity

(1) Everyone has the right to life and bodily integrity.

(2) Everyone has the right to remain free (personal freedom).

(3) All citizens are free to reside anywhere in, move throughout, enter, and leave the Territory.

(4) Capital and corporal punishment are abolished.

(5) Torture is prohibited.

Article 29 Property Integrity and Related Rights

(1) Everyone has the right to acquire, own, possess, exclusively use, and convey private property.

(2) Property may not be taken without due compensation.

Article 30 Right to Testify and Inherit

Everyone has the right to testify and inherit.

Section II Religious Freedom

Article 31 Freedom of Religion and Belief

(1) Everyone has the right to choose and practice his or her religion, creed, conscience, faith, confession, and belief.

(2) Everyone can refuse to give religious instructions.

(3) Everyone can, on the basis of conscience, refuse to serve in armed forces.

Section III Freedom of Communication

Article 32 Freedom of Expression and Information

(1) Everyone has the right to freely express and disseminate his or her opinions.

(2) The Freedom of the press and other media is guaranteed.

(3) Everyone has the right to freely retrieve information from publicly available sources.

(4) Censorship is abolished.

Article 33 Right to Assemble and Associate

(1) Everyone has the right to peacefully assemble.

(2) Everyone has the right to associate with others. This includes association in political parties.

(3) Every adult has the right to marry one partner.

Article 34 Right to Privacy

(1) Everyone has the right to privacy.

(2) The home is inviolable.

(3) The privacy of letters as well as the secrecy of mail and telecommunication are inviolable.

Section IV Freedom of Profession and Activities

Article 35 Freedom of Profession

(1) All citizens have the right to freely choose their occupation, their place of work, and their place of study or training.

(2) There is no duty to work. Forced labor is prohibited.

Article 36 Freedom of Research, Science, and Teaching

(1) Everyone has the right to research and conduct science.

(2) Everyone has the right to perform arts.

(3) Everyone has the right to teach and to found private schools.

Section V Political Rights

Article 37 Electoral Rights

(1) All resident adults have the equal right to vote and to be elected. In national elections, only citizens have this right.

(2) There is no compulsory voting.

(3) Anyone who has attained the age of eighteen years is an adult.

Article 38 Right to Petition

Everyone has the right to address written petitions to the competent agencies, to governments, and to parliaments.

Article 39 Freedom of Citizenship

(1) Citizens can at any time give up their citizenship.

(2) Citizens may at no time be forced to give up their citizenship.

Article 40 Right to Self-Determination and Resistance

(1) Everyone has the right to collective self-determination including the right to decide about membership in regional or local entities.

The State guarantees these rights through adequate powers of decentralized regional and local governments.

(2) All citizens have the right to civil disobedience and resistance against attempts to abolish this constitutional order, should no other remedy be available.

Article 41 Right to Found Political Parties

(1) Everyone has the right to found political parties respecting the principles of secularity, sovereignty, and democracy.

(2) Everyone is free to carry on politcal activities in or with such parties.

Section VI Other Liberties

Article 42 Freedom of Procreation and Childrearing

(1) Everyone has the right to procreation.

(2) Parents have the right to bringing up and educating their children. They have the right to decide about their children's participation in religious instructions.

Part III Equality

Article 43 Equality

(1) All humans are equal before the law (general equality).

(2) Matrimonial equality and legitimacy equality are guaranteed.

(3) All citizens are equally eligible for public office according to their professional aptitude.

Article 44 Prohibition of Discrimination and Privileges

(1) No person may be discriminated against or privileged on the basis of sex, gender, origin, race, language, origin, parentage, creed, faith, or nobility.

(2) Measures for the advancement of persons are admissible to remedy past discrimination (affirmative action).

Article 45 Abolishment of Nobility

No title of nobility is granted by the State. Titles of nobility are no longer part of the family name.

Part IV Right to Protection

Article 46 Special Protection

(1) Protection of human dignity is a duty of the State.

(2) The institution of marriage has the special protection of the State.

(3) Families, mothers, and minors have the special protection of the State.

(4) Everyone persecuted on political grounds has the right to asylum.

Part V Welfare Rights

Article 47 Special Support

(1) Everyone has the right to livelihood, health care, shelter, and education.

(2) Mothers have the special support of the State.

Part VI Procedural Rights

Article 48 Access to courts

(1) Everyone has free recourse to the courts.

(2) Everyone has the right to a constitutional judge. Extraordinary courts are not allowed.

(3) Persons and groups have recourse to the court acting for other rightholders not being in a position to seek relief in their own name (third party standing).

Article 49 Fair Trial

(1) Everyone has the right to a fair trial. Evidence obtained illegally is inadmissible. Everyone has the right of access to all state information required for the exercise or protection of any of his or her rights (file access).

(2) Everyone has the right to trial by jury.

(3) No one may be deprived of life, liberty, or property without due process of law.

(4) No law shall be passed stipulating regulations of the past without due compensation for all losses (ex post facto law).

Mohammad Bahareth

Article 50 Criminal Justice

(1) No act may be punished unless it constituted a criminal offence under the law before having been committed (nulla poena sine lege). No one may be punished for the same act more than once (double jeopardy).

(2) Only judges may indict or subpoena persons or issue warrants for arrest, search, or seizure.

(3) Everyone accused or arrested enjoys the right

(a) to a speedy and public trial,

(b) to be presumed innocent until proven guilty,

(c) not to be a witness against himself,

(d) promptly to be informed about the reason of accusation or detention and about the right to be silent (Miranda rights),

(e) to counsel for defence,

(f) to communicate with next-of-kin, partner, and legal, medical, and religious counsellor,

(g) to be released no later than 24 hours after the arrest if not further detended after court hearing, and

(h) to redress in case of false imprisonment.

Article 51 Prohibition of Extradition

No citizen may be extradited to a foreign country.

Chapter V Individual Restrictions

Part I General Provisions

Article 52 Admissible Restrictions

(1) The State can apply restrictions on individual rights only for the purpose of protecting individual rights of other persons or furthering other state interests explicitly mentioned in this Constitution (constitutional interest).

(2) Any restriction on individual rights must be competent and narrowly tailored to further the constitutional interest. Such restriction must be an adequate means to achieve the purpose of furthering the constitutional interest. In no case may the essence of a fundamental right be infringed.

(3) Any restriction must apply generally and not solely to an individual case.

Article 53 Special Restrictions

(1) Possession and use of drugs resulting in strong and imminent danger for the general public is prohibited.

(2) Possession and use of firearms and other weapons without a permit is prohibited.

Part II Duties

Article 54 General Duties

(1) Parents have the duty to rear and educate their minor children.

(2) Adults have the duty to support and assist their parents if they are in need.

(3) Parents and children have the duty to ensure that minors attend public schools or equivalent institutions (compulsory schooling).

Vocational schools and certified private schools are equivalent to public schools.

Article 55 Civil Service

(1) Every citizen of age serves one year in the Armed Forces, in the unarmed civil services, or in equivalent non-profit services.

(2) Whoever is unable to serve is liable to compensate the community.

Part III Burdens

Article 56 Taxation

(1) The State levies taxes from the citizens.

(2) The State levies taxes throughout the Territory.

Article 57 Mandatory Insurance

The State establishes the requirements for mandatory insurance.

Part IV State Monopolies

Article 58 Monopolies on objects

No one but the State may own heavy weapons or ultra-hazardous material.

Article 59 Monopolies on activities

(1) No one but the State may coin or print money.

(2) The State retains the monopoly on mail and telecommunication networks.

Part V Forfeiture of Fundamental Rights

Article 60 Forfeiture of Rights

(1) Persons and political parties who abuse fundamental rights in order to combat the free democratic basic order forfeit these rights.

(2) Such forfeiture and the extent thereof is determined by the Supreme Court.

Article 61 Deprivation of Electoral Rights

By final court order, the right to vote and to be elected can, partially or at large, temporarily or unlimited, be suspended if an adult

a) Has not the requisite mental capacity for any legal responsibility or

b) Has irrevocably been sentenced to at least one year of imprisonment.